FORTY YEARS OF AMERICAN-JAPANESE RELATIONS

by

FOSTER RHEA DULLES

Author of "America in the Pacific," etc.

D. APPLETON-CENTURY COMPANY
INCORPORATED
NEW YORK   LONDON
1937

A T RECURRENT INTERVALS DURING THE PAST FORTY years, the relations between America and Japan have become so strained as to lead to widespread talk of the possibility of war. Popular feeling on either side of the Pacific has flared up dangerously over an apparent clash of interests for whose settlement the extremists have demanded the arbitrament of force.

The basic cause for this recurrent friction in the past, the potential source of future controversy, is found in a single set of circumstances. Our traditional Far Eastern policy in support of the Open Door and the territorial integrity of China directly conflicts with Japan's deep-seated ambition for overseas expansion and the establishment of unquestioned political and economic supremacy over all of Eastern Asia. At times this underlying conflict has been intensified by bitter controversy over the issue of Japanese immigration in the United States, and at times it has been ominously reflected in the development of intense naval rivalry in the Pacific. But the status of China remains the crux of the Far Eastern problem.

The policy that has led America to become deeply involved in the political relations of the Orient stands out as one of the most unusual and paradoxical phenomena in our national life. Toward Europe we have consistently maintained, except for the brief and tragic interlude of the World War, an attitude of aloofness which has enabled us to avoid any serious entanglements. But we have not hesitated, again and again, to intervene directly in the affairs of Eastern Asia. Even the certainty that such action would arouse the resentment and hostility of Japan has not served to keep us at home.

At the same time, we have never sought to carry such intervention in the Far East to the point where it could effectively attain our declared objectives of upholding the Open Door and safeguarding China's independence. Our policy has not conformed to the realities of the situations in which we have attempted to intervene. In striking contrast to the popular support that Japan's program has always been able to command among her own people, American policy has not had the essential backing of a popular determination to uphold it by force. We have consequently made bold declarations of policy whose possible effect has invariably been nullified by enforced inaction; we have advanced aggressively in defense of our interests, and on sober second thought have beat a cautious retreat.

Within the past year enactment of the neutrality law has injected an entirely new factor into this situation, with implications which can hardly be reconciled with our historic policy or with certain of the treaty obligations we have assumed, and the general apathy of the American public toward further Japanese encroachments on Chinese independence has afforded additional evidence of what would appear to be a complete withdrawal from the Far East. Nevertheless, renewed conflict between China and Japan, signalized by the clash of their military forces in the summer of 1937, brings up problems which cannot be dismissed on the specious grounds that Asia is too distant for its quarrels to be of any direct concern to the United States. We are again confronted with the vital question of just what policy this country should follow in the face of present-day realities of war and peace in the Orient.

This study makes no attempt to suggest our future policy. It is an account of our political relations with Japan since 1898, of the controversies and disputes that give to that relationship such an outstanding importance. But as the story unfolds, it graphically reveals the decline of American influence and prestige in the Far East before the relentless growth of Japanese political and economic power. It becomes a record of the practical failure of the policy popularly symbolized by the Open Door.

F. R. D.

CONTENTS

ILLUSTRATIONS

AMERICA AND JAPAN

CHAPTER I

IMPERIALISM

IN THE LAST DECADE OF THE NINETEENTH CENTURY, imperialism was in full flood. It was an era of economic and political expansion which placed no limits upon national ambitions. In bland disregard of national rights and in jealous rivalry of one another, the Powers were prepared to divide among themselves whatever territories could be brought under their political or economic control. In the Far East a determined struggle was under way over the prostrate form of China.

For many years the centuries-old Middle Kingdom had been subjected to the persistent encroachments of the West, and under this relentless pressure the Manchu régime had become thoroughly demoralized. Its complete collapse appeared imminent. After 1895 the only question at issue, in the chancelleries of Europe, was whether Great Britain, Russia, Germany, or France would secure a more valuable share of the division of the spoils. "The various powers cast upon us looks of tiger-like voracity," exclaimed the redoubtable old Empress Dowager who sat upon the Dragon Throne, "hustling each other in their endeavors to be the first to seize upon our innermost territories."

On the opposite shores of the Pacific, America and Japan appeared for a time to stand apart from this mad scramble. Japan had attempted to anticipate Europe, had indeed seized the island of Formosa, but she had been repulsed in her ambition to win additional territory by a concert of the Powers which forced her to disgorge the larger part of the plunder from her war with China in 1894. Not yet strong enough to assert what she considered her rights, she was forced to stand aside as a jealous but impotent spectator of the intrigues of Western imperialism.

America at the same time held aloof, not because she was too weak to gratify whatever ambitions she might have had, but because her strength and boundless natural resources appeared to preclude any need for overseas expansion. We kept out of the race of imperialism for a time, allowed Europe to quarrel over China, because we had no desire to acquire territory in so distant a part of the world.

Before the century drew to a final close, however, America gave a striking demonstration that she too was anything but immune to the virus of imperialism, and soon thereafter events clearly showed that thwarted Japan had been merely hoarding her strength. The observer who before 1898 might have judged from the quiescent attitude of America and Japan that these two Powers had permanently forsworn expansion, and would play no rôle in the rivalries of Far Eastern imperialism, was doomed to be rudely disillusioned.

A substantial background for both American and Japanese imperialism, indeed, could have been discovered by any reading of history. In the case of this country, the idea that no other Power should be allowed to establish dominion in the Pacific or exclusive control of its commerce may be traced back over a century. It played its part in the first efforts made to reach the Western Ocean and in the founding of our early trade with China. It was one of the forces making for the overland movement and the acquisition of Oregon and California. American settlements on the West Coast were urged as a means to forestall the insidious attempt of Great Britain "to fence us out from the Pacific." In the debates on the Oregon question and in the bitter discussion which rose out of the Mexican War, the need to safeguard our position in the Pacific and the Far East was urged with all the eloquence which the exponents of expansion could command.

We would have gone further and established insular outposts if the more ambitious expansionists could have had their way. As early as 1842 the possibility of the Kingdom of Hawaii being subjected to foreign control had been viewed with grave foreboding by President Tyler. As Secretary of State, Daniel Webster declared that "we might even feel justified, consistently with our own principles, in interfering by force to prevent its falling into the hands of one of the great powers of Europe." Some ten years later a treaty of annexation was actually concluded with the island government, solely with the idea of strengthening our position in the Pacific and protecting the trade route to the Orient.

Upon the occasion of his visit to Japan about this same time, Commodore Perry also recommended the acquisition of Formosa and the Liuchiu Islands. "It is self-evident," this imperialistic naval officer wrote in a remarkable dispatch penned in 1852, "that the course of coming events will ere long make it necessary for the United States to extend its jurisdiction beyond the limits of the western continent, and I assume the responsibility of urging the expediency of establishing a foothold in this quarter of the globe, as a measure of positive necessity to the sustainment of our maritime rights in the East."

President Lincoln's Secretary of State, William H. Seward, was equally convinced of the necessity of some such action, in the firm belief that the Pacific was destined to become the "chief theatre of events in the world's great hereafter." He strongly favored annexation of Hawaii, suggested that we might seek a naval base off the China coast, and in 1867 made one successful move to give practical effect to his program of expansion in the Pacific. This was the purchase of Alaska. Its mineral resources unknown, popularly considered a wholly barren and inhospitable country, Seward could justify the acquisition of Alaska only on the grounds that it constituted "a drawbridge between America and Asia."

Following the Civil War, the absorption of the country in the immense task of developing the West effectually prevented any further overseas expansion. Our ties with Hawaii were strengthened; we established a certain measure of control over the Samoan Islands; and occasional voices preached the nebulous goal of "mastery of the Pacific." But renewal of our real advance toward Asia awaited the startling events of the Spanish War.

This conflict grew out of our somewhat self-righteous

and impetuous desire to free Cuba from the tyranny of Spanish rule. Possible repercussions in the Pacific were foreseen by only a handful of starry-eyed enthusiasts in Washington who were chafing under America's reluctance to join the march of world imperialism. They had duly noted that the Philippine Islands were a Spanish possession, and that here was an opportunity to obtain a makeweight for any division of China among the European nations. The dispatch from Commodore Dewey on May 1, 1898, announcing that he had defeated the Spanish fleet in Manila Bay and was in control of the Philippines, was for them a siren call to the realization of a still greater "manifest destiny" than that envisaged half a century earlier.

"The booming guns of Dewey's battle-ships sounded a new note on the Pacific shores," enthusiastically declared one Congressman in this vanguard of American imperialism, "a note that has echoed and reëchoed around the world, and that note is that we are on the Pacific, that we are there to stay, and that we are there to protect our rights, promote our interests, and get our share of the trade and commerce of the opulent Orient."

The possible implications of Dewey's victory were not so quickly realized by the public. The American people were to prove willing disciples of the new imperialism. They were to take up enthusiastically the white man's burden. But for a time they floundered in a sea of indecision. And well they might. For as Mr. Dooley sagely remarked to Mr. Hennissy, in discussing the novel proposal that we should take over the Philippines,

" 'Tis not more thin two months since ye larned whether they were islands or canned goods."

President McKinley reflected the doubts and indecisions of his countrymen as the more determined expansionists brought their pressure to bear upon him. He wrestled with his conscience; he sought Divine light and guidance. But gradually whatever scruples he had in regard to America's right to annex the Philippines as a consequence of a war undertaken to free Cuba were worn away by the inexorable logic of economic imperialism.

McKinley became the instrument of a force greater than himself. America had reached a point in her economic development where an apparent surplus of both capital and goods demanded foreign outlets. Finance looked to investment abroad; industry sought foreign markets. Eastern Asia appeared the most promising field for economic expansion. If the European countries were to control China, some base of operations in the Western Pacific was a vital necessity.

"If it is commercialism to want the possession of a strategic point giving the American people an opportunity to maintain a foothold in the markets of that great Eastern country," the blunt and forthright Mark Hanna declared, "for God's sake let us have commercialism."

Moreover it was a larger question than immediate markets: political control of the Pacific appeared to be at stake. America could no longer stand aside. Captain Alfred Thayer Mahan, enthusiastic spokesman for the influence of sea-power upon history, had been urging America "to look outward." It was vital for this country, he stated, to carry its life "beyond the borders which heretofore have sufficed for its activities." We had "an imperative need for an impregnable defensive position in the Pacific."

For a time the President thought that the retention of one of the Philippine Islands would meet the needs of commerce and naval strategy. But the popular feeling developed that in the interests of the Filipinos themselves, as well as for the sake of peace in the Far East, all the islands should be retained. McKinley had to re-examine his views. Finally he convinced himself, in what was unquestionably a sincere rationalization of the imperialistic ambitions which were sweeping the country, that it was our moral duty "to educate the Filipinos, and uplift and civilize and Christianize them, and by God's grace do the very best we could by them."

Upon this the decision was made. The American delegates at the peace conference in Paris were instructed to demand the cession of all the Islands. Public opinion emphatically approved. "Whether on the side of the angels or not," one acute observer noted, "the Administration was keeping step with what the majority of the American people desired."

This is not to say that there were not horrified voices raised in protest. A militant minority both in Congress and outside its halls vigorously fought what it regarded as a betrayal of our traditional democracy. Imperialism and colonial expansion had no place in the American scheme of things, according to these dissenting elements. When the ungrateful Filipinos showed a distressing lack of appreciation of our efforts to aid them, the anti-imperialists grew more and more scornful of our gratuitous assumption of the white man's burden.

"Underneath the starry flag, civilize him with a Krag," ran a popular verse. When Commissioner William Howard Taft spoke affectionately of our "little brown brother," sardonic voices sang.

> He may be a brother of Big Bill Taft
> But he ain't no brother of mine.

Nevertheless the country as a whole shouldered its new responsibilities with zest. It welcomed the opportunity to extend to less fortunate people the benefits of American institutions and social customs, and accepted imperialism as both inevitable and highly desirable in an imperialistic world.

Nor should it be forgotten that the acquisition of the Philippines was only one phase of the expansion so unexpectedly ushered in by the Spanish-American War. The long pending treaty of annexation with Hawaii was impatiently set aside in the opening days of the war to enable Congress to assert title to these mid-Pacific islands through a joint resolution. We took possession of one of the Samoan Islands as the result of a tripartite agreement negotiated with Great Britain and Germany. And on their way to the Philippines, the American troops went a little out of their way to seize Spain's island colony of Guam—to the startled bewilderment of the Spanish officials who did not even know that their country was at war.

America had suddenly become a World Power. In the excitement of the period, amazing statements were made as to the great future now opening up before the country. The Philippines were to assure our domination of the trade of the Orient. They were to make possible our unquestioned political supremacy throughout the Pacific area. We were to go forth as world conquerors. "This is what fate holds for the chosen people," wrote William Allen White. "It is so written—it is to be."

No spokesman of the new era was more eloquent than the young Senator from Indiana, Albert J. Beveridge. He recognized in our imperialism "the unseen hand of God." Upon his return from a visit to the Philippines, an eager country awaited his verdict upon what possession of the islands might mean in fulfilling our high destiny. Nor was it disappointed.

"The Philippines are ours forever," Senator Beveridge told a crowded Senate in a speech which made front page head-lines from coast to coast, ". . . And just beyond the Philippines are China's illimitable markets. We will not retreat from either. We will not repudiate our duty in the archipelago. We will not abandon our duty in the Orient. We will not renounce our part in the mission of our race, trustee, under God, of the civilization of the world. . . . Our largest trade henceforth must be with Asia. The Pacific is our ocean . . . and the Pacific is the ocean of the commerce of the future. Most future wars will be conflicts for commerce. The Power that rules the Pacific, therefore, is the Power that rules the world. And, with the Philippines, that Power is and will forever be the American Republic."

It was magnificent. Never had the country heard such oratory. "Ye could waltz to it," declared the irrepressible Mr. Dooley. And for a brief interlude, which in later years was to appear strangely unreal, that was just about what the country did.

The course of Japanese imperialism during the latter half of the nineteenth century presented a quite different picture from that of American imperialism. It did not undergo such a sudden, dramatic development; it was more a matter of steady, persistent growth. Nor was it to come to its full fruition until a considerably later period.

Prior to the birth of modern Japan, the history of the country had been marked by a degree of international isolation for which the modern world offers no parallel. Under the rule of the Tokugawa shogunate, the military power which exercised dominant control while the Mikado existed only as a shadowy symbol, Japan enjoyed for two and a half centuries both internal and external peace. The former because the shoguns had welded the feudal clans into an integrated whole owing loyalty to themselves; the latter because it was forbidden the Japanese to have any contact with the outside world.

In the sixteenth and early seventeenth centuries Europeans had visited Japan. The Jesuit priests had made thousands of Christian converts; British and Dutch traders had established a thriving commerce. But they had been driven out of the country when the great Iyeyasu decided they constituted a disturbing element within the kingdom. Except for a Dutch post at Deshima, Japan was hermetically sealed against foreign intrusion, and until 1854 her society evolved uninfluenced by association with the Western World.

In this early history, however, two considerations may serve to foreshadow the course which Japan adopted when circumstances no longer permitted her to exist in complete isolation. "Almost the whole of authentic Japanese history," Lafcadio Hearn has written, "is comprised in one vast episode: the rise and fall of the military power." The struggle between civil and military government within the Japanese Empire is thus no new phenomenon. While loyalty to the Emperor has survived all changes, the failure of any government to satisfy the military traditions of the Japanese people has inevitably led to its overthrow.

Also in that period toward the close of the sixteenth century when Hideyoshi, another of the great figures of Japanese history, was attempting to consolidate the country, he had recourse to the useful expedient of imperialistic aggression. An unprovoked war was declared against Korea to the end that it might serve as a base for the further conquest of China. While this war dragged on unsatisfactorily until Hideyoshi's death six years later and the Japanese troops were then recalled, here is precedent for ambitions flowering again after a lapse of almost three and a half centuries.

Upon emergence from her period of isolation, a move made primarily upon the insistent bidding of the United States, Japan found herself, in 1854, alone and helpless in a world which had long since passed her by in all material development. There were far-sighted Japanese statesmen even in that day, however, who realized that the only way in which their country could win the respect of other nations, and establish its position in the Far East, was to make over Japanese civilization along

the lines followed by the West. This meant industrialization, the encouragement of foreign trade, scientific progress, and modern armaments. It also meant, in self-
defense if not for self-aggrandizement, national expansion as the nations of the West had expanded.

For such a program the Japanese people showed a remarkable adaptability. The demands of military security, the need for raw materials and foreign markets,
the pressure of an increasing population imprisoned in
the narrow confines of a small island kingdom, all played
their part in the creation of Japanese imperialism. But
possibly more important than any external factor, than
all the laws of economic determinism, were certain
racial attributes. The abounding vitality of the Japanese, their ambition, and their proud faith in their
national destiny, drove them forward on an irresistible
course.

The principles upon which Japan should act were
set forth only four years after the epochal visit of the
"black ships" of Commodore Perry. In a significant
memorial submitted to the Throne in 1858, Lord Hotta,
Councilor of State and Prime Minister, urged his countrymen to set about remedying their defects in any
particular in which they found themselves excelled by
foreigners. Shipping and trade should be promoted, national resources should be developed, military preparations should be made. Where other nations intervened,
Lord Hotta declared, Japan should do the same. In
even more emphatic terms, he stated that "the object
should always be kept in view of laying the foundation
for securing hegemony over all nations."

Moreover, this Japanese minister, who so early

learned the lessons of imperialism and forecast his country's policy toward China and Korea, accepted such expansion as a duty laid upon Japan by a higher Power. In phraseology not unlike that employed by Senator Beveridge almost half a century later, he, too, recognized in his country's national destiny "the unseen hand of God."

"Such a policy," Lord Hotta said, "could be nothing else but enforcement of the power and authority deputed to us by the Spirit of Heaven. Our national prestige and position thus assured, the nations of the world will come to look up to our Emperor as the Great Ruler of all the nations, and they will come to follow our policy and submit themselves to our judgment."

It was a difficult path for Japan to follow. Her own independence was at stake in the first years of her emergence from isolation. She found herself hemmed in and baffled by the encroachments of the Powers in their rivalry to dominate her trade. It came to be more and more widely realized that a long period of training in the ways of the West, and a great increase in armaments, were necessary before Japan could even win freedom from the extraterritorial and special tariff privileges which the Powers had exacted of her.

So we find in 1887 another Japanese leader recalling the ambitions which Lord Hotta had first voiced, but counseling patience and moderation. "Make our country secure by military preparation," declared Viscount Tani. ". . . Encourage and protect the people at home, and then wait for the time of the confusion of Europe which must come eventually sooner or later, and although we have no immediate concern with it ourselves we must feel it, for such an event will agitate the nations of the Orient as well, and hence, although our country is not mixed up in the matter, so far as Europe is concerned, we may then become the chief nation of the Orient."

Japan in the meantime did not neglect such opportunities as came her way to strengthen and consolidate her power in the Far East. There were the Liuchiu Islands, whose annexation by the United States had been suggested by Commodore Perry. For long, title to them had been in dispute between Japan and China, but by 1879 they were definitely incorporated in the former nation. So, too, with the Bonin Islands, another small group off the coast of Japan whose title of ownership was obscure and in which Great Britain had shown some interest. An abortive expedition to Formosa and a dispute with Russia over Sakhalin offered further evidence that, in so far as she could, Japan was building an empire.

A more important objective, even in these early days, was expansion on the Asiatic mainland. Japan could not be indifferent to conditions in Manchuria and Korea; they could too easily threaten the peace and stability of the near-by kingdom. Just when actual control of these territories first became a definite objective of the Japanese Government cannot be stated, but no sooner had Korea, the Hermit Kingdom, been opened to foreign intercourse than Japan was intriguing to undermine Chinese influence and forestall Russian penetration in this unprogressive, effete, and impotent country.

This policy was a logical if not an inevitable development. Apart from strategic reasons, the mainland offered
the most promising field for commercial expansion, and
Japan could hardly be expected to stand aside if opportunity beckoned. Her only fault, as Japanese apologists
have been reiterating for more than a third of a century,
was that she was entering the race of imperialism too
late. The field was overcrowded.

The conflict of interests in Korea soon led to a direct
clash between China and Japan. It was clearly evident
that the Korean Government could not maintain internal peace and order, and when in 1894 Japan determined to substitute her influence for that exercised
by China as Korea's nominal suzerain, war flared up.
It was hard-fought and brief. To the astonishment of
the West, which had hardly realized what tremendous
forward strides she had made in modern warfare, Japan
quickly overwhelmed her ponderous foe.

The terms of peace clearly revealed Japan's ambitions. Recognition of complete independence for Korea
brought to an end Chinese influence at the Korean
capital; the island of Formosa was ceded to the victors;
and China agreed to award Japan a territorial base on
the Asiatic mainland through the cession of the Liao-
tung Peninsula in Southern Manchuria.

But it was at this point the European Powers stepped
in. Japan was going ahead too fast. A territorial base
in Manchuria interfered with their own plans for the
possible division of the now patently moribund Chinese
Empire. Acting in close concert, Russia, Germany, and
France advised the Japanese Government not to insist
upon territorial cessions on the mainland.

Japan could do nothing other than accept this advice. It was clear that the Powers meant business and that they would not allow her to disregard their "friendly" counsel. And without allies, she was far too weak to challenge their interference. The peace treaty already signed was modified by an agreement to return Liao-tung to China.

So Japan's first vigorous advance along the road of imperialism was halted far short of its goal. A disappointed people realized that they had to build up national strength to a far greater extent before Japan could hope to play the rôle in the Far East which they felt was her imperial destiny. As the European Powers proceeded to carve China into foreign spheres of influence, plans which embraced Russia's seizure of the very territory she had forced this imperialistic interloper to surrender, Japan reluctantly adopted the policy of "an innocent onlooker in foreign relations."

It was only a pose. Once again a far-sighted statesman may be found voicing the real attitude of Japan. Count Tadasu Hayashi, the future author of the Anglo-Japanese Alliance, soberly advised his countrymen to learn the lessons of history.

"What Japan has now to do," he wrote in 1895, "is to keep perfectly quiet, to lull the suspicions that have arisen against her, and to wait, meanwhile strengthening the foundations of her national power, watching and waiting for the opportunity which must one day surely come in the Orient. When that day arrives she will be able to follow her own course, not only able to put meddling powers in their places, but even, as necessity arises, meddling with the affairs of other powers.

Then truly she will be able to reap advantages for herself."

In this forward movement of American and Japanese imperialism in the closing years of the nineteenth century, triumphant on the part of America, abruptly checked in the case of Japan, the two nations had not clashed. The conflict in their aims and aspirations had not materialized. Their common objective, although their methods of seeking to attain it might differ, was to prevent the European Powers from establishing so dominant a position in the Far East that their own political and commercial interests would be endangered.

In their relations with each other, indeed, America and Japan were bound by the most close and cordial ties. This country had played the leading rôle in opening up Japan, and in their dealings with the Japanese authorities, both Commodore Perry and Townsend Harris, our first consul-general, had laid the basis for what appeared to be an enduring international friendship. In his treaty negotiations in 1858, Harris had exhibited a sincere concern to safeguard the best interests of Japan as well as to promote those of his own country. The concessions he made stood the confused and perplexed Japanese in good stead in their subsequent negotiations with the other Powers.

In the inevitable controversies between Japan and the West, conflicts in which Japanese domestic problems were inextricably involved, the influence of the United States was almost invariably conciliatory. While on one occasion we took part in a military expedition to enforce respect for foreign rights, there was never a time during the nineteenth century when Japan did not realize that America was her most certain friend in the strange world into which she had been so suddenly projected.

By 1870, moreover, American policy was entirely divorced from the more aggressive policies pursued by the European Powers. We took an independent lead in promoting a revision of the original treaties Japan had signed with the West along lines which would assure her full equality in the family of nations. We were prepared to abolish extraterritoriality and concede tariff autonomy before any other Power would consider such a basic change in its relations with a Far Eastern nation. If we followed such a course because we were convinced it was really to our advantage to do so, it was nevertheless true that we acted in Japan's interest as well as our own.

Not until about 1894, when America first undertook to annex the Hawaiian Islands as a prelude to its Pacific advance four years later, did any question arise of the possibility of conflicting ambitions. Japan then protested the proposed annexation. The Tokyo Government declared that it could not view without concern such a change in the status quo in the Pacific. But this protest was soon withdrawn. Japan was ready to recognize American control in Hawaii in view of the distinctly friendly attitude we showed toward her during her war with China.

The United States on this occasion refused to approve a vague project for foreign intervention which had for its objective a Western guarantee of the independence of Korea. British overtures in behalf of such a move were rejected on the ground that such action would not be in the best interest of either China or Japan. And we warned Japan of the distinct danger that the military Powers might intervene should she attempt to obtain territorial concessions on the Asiatic mainland. "It is not impossible," stated the American note, "that other powers having interests in that quarter may demand a settlement not favorable to Japan's future security and well-being."

In recognition of these signs that America and Japan were at one in opposing the extension of European influence in the Far East, the Japanese Government offered no opposition to American acquisition of the Philippines in 1898. If Japan had been in a position to seize the islands herself, it might have been a different matter. Under the circumstances prevailing at the close of the century, she welcomed rather than resented the definite entry of the United States into Far Eastern politics.

Proof of this attitude was afforded by an interview which Senator Beveridge had with Premier Ito upon the occasion of the former's visit to the Far East in the summer of 1899. This leading statesman of the new Japan emphatically advised the young American Senator that the United States should retain the Philippines because "your national honor is involved; because it is to your interest, not at once, but greatly, almost incontestably so in the future; and because, if you do not, another Power will immediately take them, involving the world in war in all probability."

America did not necessarily want Japan to control Korea and Manchuria; Japan did not necessarily want

America to control Hawaii and the Philippines. But each nation preferred to see the other established in these territories rather than any European Power. They did not anticipate their own intense rivalry. Japan saw no danger in the United States strengthening its influence and power in the Pacific; America recognized no threat to her interests in Japanese expansion on the Asiatic mainland.

CHAPTER II

THE OPEN DOOR

WITH THE PHILIPPINE ISLANDS SERVING AS AN OUT-
post of American power and influence in the
Pacific, the United States was not long in taking
a further step to achieve the objectives which consciously or unconsciously had motivated our imperialistic policy. For protection of our trade in the Far East
demanded something more than establishment of a
naval base off the coast of China. If the expected break-
up of the Chinese Empire should actually take place, it
was essential to secure guarantees that American rights
would not be prejudiced.

The move we now made was little more than a formulation of the general policy we had followed in the Far
East throughout the nineteenth century. It was very
limited in its scope. It was by no means entirely successful. Nevertheless, advocacy of the Open Door in China
has proved to be one of the most momentous pronounce-
ments of foreign policy this country has ever made. Its
far-reaching implications have ever since had a vital influence in the history of the Far East. This is true not
because the Open Door has been accepted by the world
—it has always been a doctrine more honored in the
breach than the observance—but because it has so
deeply involved us in the Far East and recurrently

brought us in dangerous conflict with Japanese imperialism.

At the time, due to Tokyo's adoption of the policy of "an innocent onlooker in foreign relations," these later developments could not be foreseen. For the Open Door policy was definitely directed against European and not Japanese encroachments upon China. Even more specifically, it was directed against Russian activities in Manchuria. Its objective was the maintenance of commercial equality in a part of the world where America felt herself being frozen out of opportunities for trade and investment which were considered of great potential importance.

Japan naturally enough warmly welcomed the Open Door policy. Still too weak to prevent the steady infiltration of Russian influence in Manchuria, any program which would serve to bar the Czarist advance was greatly to her advantage. If it did not actually strengthen her own position, it would at least hold her rival in check. Japan was working for time. If some day she hoped to take more active and energetic measures to secure control of Manchuria for herself, our stand might preserve the coveted territory from complete foreign absorption until she was ready to strike.

In the negotiations in regard to the Open Door, Japan consequently played a minor rôle. She was in a certain sense a silent and sympathetic partner of the United States. It is one of the ironies of history that in so far as our policy at the close of the past century succeeded in preventing the complete break-up of China, it did so only to preserve that unfortunate country, on the basis of events some thirty years later, for subsequent aggression on the part of Japan.

The development of this policy is closely linked with the development of our trade with China or, more specifically, with hopes and expectations for that trade which have never been fully realized.

This commerce began almost immediately after the Revolution. The American colonies had been greatly dependent upon the triangular trade with Africa and the West Indies in slaves and rum, but with independence it was closed to them by the British navigation laws. New ports had to be discovered, new trade routes developed, if political independence was not to prove a barren victory. And among the first markets sought out to meet this challenge to the mercantile enterprise of the lusty young Republic were those of China.

The year in which George Washington was elected the first President of the United States saw fifteen American vessels lading teas and silks from the musty godowns at Canton. Ships from New York, Boston, Philadelphia, and Salem, which a few years before had been preying upon British commerce in the Atlantic, were boldly cutting into the trade hitherto monopolized by the great East India Company. They rounded Cape Horn, cruised along the rocky shore of the Northwest Coast, braved the treacherous shoals of the South Sea Islands, in a zealous quest for products to exchange for those of China.

The canny Yankee seamen of the Atlantic seaports found traders after their own hearts in the shrewd merchants of the Canton hong. Americans and Chinese

got along famously in these early days. "All Chinaman
very much love your country," Samuel Shaw, elected by
Congress to serve as our first consul in Canton, was told
by one of the hong merchants. In turn he gave his
opinion that the Chinese traders "are as respectable a
set of men as are commonly found in other parts of the
world."

But while there was no conflict between Americans
and Chinese in Canton, a controversy over the importation of opium led to a clash between the Chinese authorities and the British in 1840. There was a concen-
tration of naval vessels; hostilities broke out; and England undertook to compel China to place the trade at
Canton on a firmer basis and to open additional ports
to foreign shipping. The Americans, as they were to do
on many subsequent occasions, stood carefully apart
from this quarrel. But they were none the less determined that any concessions the British might obtain
should also be extended to them. Commodore Lawrence
Kearny, an American naval officer opportunely in Canton, undertook to impress this upon the Chinese.

The reply to his representations was prompt.

"Decidedly it shall not be permitted," wrote the Governor of Canton, "that the American merchants shall
come to have merely a dry stick (that is, their interests
shall be attended to) . I, the Governor, will not be otherwise disposed than to look up to the heart of the great
Emperor in his compassionate regard toward these men
from afar. . . ."

In this demand on the part of Commodore Kearny
and the somewhat cryptic response of the Governor of
Canton, there was vaguely formulated the basic proposi-

tion of our traditional policy in the Far East. Their exchange of notes postulated the principle to be embodied a few years later in our first treaty with China, and subsequently in every treaty. This principle was that America was entitled to the same treatment in her trade and commerce with China as that accorded to the most favored nation—under any and all circumstances.

Recognition of such rights was considered very important in America. The trade with China had played a major rôle in reviving the commerce of New England; it had brought prosperity to many an Atlantic port. As a representative of the country's shipping interests, Secretary of State Webster duly instructed our first envoy to the Far East to make it clear that the United States would find it impossible to remain on terms of friendship with China if her government ever granted greater privileges to the citizens of any other country than she did to those of the United States.

Apart from the actualities of our trade with China, this early period also saw the birth of that mystical, romantic belief in the unlimited possibilities of commerce with the Far East which has ever since exercised its incredible hold upon popular imagination. American tobacco was to replace opium; American wheat and rice were to become the staples of the Orient. "All this mighty laboratory whence the world has supplied itself for fifty centuries with articles of luxury, comfort and common use," reads a contemporary document, "will pour itself forth in exchange for the produce of the Mississippi Valley."

It was a dream which did not materialize. American trade with China expanded rapidly until about 1858.

Then it began to decline. By the close of the century it had dropped from about 3 per cent of our total foreign trade to less than 2 per cent. Somewhere there had been a slip in that ambitious program wherein the East was to exchange its luxuries for the bounteous produce of the Mississippi Valley.

In 1899, the total foreign trade of China had a value about three times what it had had in the seventies, and the United States was supplying more than its quota of the rising tide of Chinese imports of cotton goods, kerosene oil, railway equipment, and other products of Western industry. Nevertheless our imports from China, valued at $18,619,000, compared with total American imports valued at $850,000,000, and exports to China, amounting to $14,493,000, were in even more marked contrast with our total exports of $1,371,000,000.

While China constituted a by no means negligible market for American goods and manufacturers, in the final analysis her markets absorbed little more than one-tenth of 1 per cent of the products of American industry, and only about 1 per cent of even such products as we actually sent abroad.

Investments in China at this time were relatively even less important than trade. American shipping in Chinese waters—in marked contrast to conditions prior to the Civil War—was almost non-existent; there were comparatively few American business firms operating in China; and American holdings of Chinese Government obligations were inconsequential. The total for all American investment in China in 1900 was estimated to amount to no more than $25,000,000, of which business investments accounted for $17,500,000, mission property for $5,000,000, and securities and Government obligations for $2,200,000.

But despite these facts and figures, the dream of expanding trade with China, that dream originally bequeathed to the West by Marco Polo, had not lost its hold upon American imagination. In the face of all realities, the Far East was still believed to proffer unlimited markets for our trade and commerce. With the growing need for new markets and new fields for investment at the close of the century, the Orient still beckoned.

The trade of China, Senator Beveridge declared, is "the mightiest commercial fact in our future." He foresaw its potentialities in almost exactly the same terms as the pamphleteers of more than half a century earlier. "That statesman commits a crime . . . against the American grower of cotton and wheat and tobacco, the American manufacturer of machinery and clothing," he proclaimed in an eloquent panegyric on the potentialities of China's markets, "who fails to put America where she can command that trade."

Throughout the nineteenth century, the teeming millions of China were invariably envisioned as just so many customers for American manufactures. And today the American mind sometimes appears to be just as easily dazzled by the fascinating picture of 400,000,000 Chinese wearing 400,000,000 pairs of American shoes, listening to 400,000,000 American radios, and driving 400,000,000 American automobiles.

It was in the light of this background that America took up, in 1899, the problem of protecting her trade

interests against any restrictive measures in the concessions or spheres of influence which the European
Powers had wrested from the Chinese Government. For
whether or not the ultimate consequence of these encroachments was to be the complete break-up of the
Empire, the commercial interests in this country were
determined not to be shut off from the Chinese market.

It was an issue which strongly appealed to the new
Secretary of State appointed by President McKinley
toward the close of 1898. No abler servant of American
industry, no firmer advocate of economic imperialism,
could have been found than John Hay. His background
was that of a liberal. He had been one of Lincoln's
secretaries; he was historian, novelist, and poet. At an
earlier period he had condemned the idea of overseas
expansion. But "our Pacific work" now appeared to
Hay to be of the greatest importance. Observing the
westward course of empire, he sententiously wrote: "No
man, no party, can fight with any chance of final success against a cosmic tendency."

Three possible courses were open to America. We
might join the scramble for territory in China, establishing our own sphere of influence or demanding the
cession of a port comparable to those held by England, Germany, and Russia. We might coöperate with
Great Britain, which was beginning to feel that further
dismemberment of China was not to her interest, in
collective action to restrain the military powers: Russia,
France, and Germany. Or finally, we might take independent action more in line with our traditional
policy in the Far East.

Against the first course, the objections were immediate and overwhelming. The evidence appears to show that President McKinley was not personally averse to the United States obtaining a slice of Chinese territory should circumstances make it advisable, but Secretary Hay had no illusions upon the practicality of such a program. For, while possession of the Philippines had momentarily whetted the national appetite for overseas territory, public opinion could in no sense be counted upon to support such an unprecedented venture as territorial expansion in China.

In regard to possible coöperative action with Great Britain, the objections were also strong. Before the Spanish-American War, Downing Street had confidentially inquired of the State Department whether the United States would join England in opposing any action by a foreign Power which tended to restrict freedom of commerce in China. It had also suggested a joint undertaking to this same effect upon the part of Great Britain, the United States, and Germany. At the time President McKinley gave these proposals little consideration as he became more and more involved in larger worries attendant upon our relations with Spain, but they had been informally revived after the war in the speeches and public statements of Lord Charles Beresford, supersalesman for British interests in the Far East.

Beresford advocated joint Anglo-American action to enforce a policy to which he gave the name of the "open door." The phrase was not his own. President McKinley himself had used it in connection with trade in the Philippine Islands. But this was its first popular application to trade with China. The British statesman strongly urged that the Open Door was even more to the interest of the United States than to that of England, and in the fall of 1898 he wrote Secretary Hay that he hoped "the suggested commercial alliance between Great Britain and America with reference to the 'open door' may become an absolute fact."

Possibly Hay might have favored such a program: he was a great Anglophile. But public opinion did not want too close ties with Great Britain. It had no liking for entangling alliances, and there was little question that such an accord would involve us deeply in European politics. The Powers were making China a stage for the interplay of their own rivalries and conflicting ambitions.

The third course open to America, that of independent action along the lines of our traditional Far Eastern policy, consequently appealed to Hay not only as the most feasible one but as the most logical. It was a program which would conform to England's desires but preserve our freedom of action. And this policy he was being strongly urged to adopt, in the summer of 1899, by two Far Eastern experts in Washington.

These men were W. W. Rockhill, a former secretary of the legation in Peking, and Alfred E. Hippesley, one time of the Chinese Customs Service. Late in July, the latter "ventured to suggest" in a note to Rockhill that the United States should officially call the attenton of the Powers to conditions in China, and seek to obtain assurance that there would be no discrimination against the trade of other nations in the territories they controlled. Five weeks later, Rockhill incorporated this idea more definitely in a memorandum forwarded to

Hay. The protection of American interests in the foreign spheres of influence, he told the Secretary of State, demanded prompt and decisive action.

Secretary Hay now acted more than promptly. Within a week he dispatched virtually identical notes to Great Britain, Germany, France, Russia, Italy, and Japan which embodied, almost without the change of a phrase, the suggestions of his advisers.

In the note addressed to Great Britain, he pointed out that the commercial communities of the two nations urgently demanded maintenance of "what is commonly called the 'open door' policy" and that the United States Government could not "conceal its apprehension" that there was danger of complications growing out of the involved situation in China which might imperil American treaty rights. To safeguard its citizens from exclusive treatment by any of the controlling Powers in their various spheres of influence, the United States consequently sought the adherence of each of the Powers to a threefold declaration of policy:

1. That it will in no wise interfere with any treaty port or any vested interest within any so-called "sphere of influence" or leased territory it may have in China.

2. That the Chinese treaty tariff of the time being shall apply to all merchandise landed or shipped to all such ports as are within such "spheres of influence" (unless they be "free ports"), no matter to what nationality it may belong, and that duties so leviable shall be collected by the Chinese Government.

3. That it will levy no higher harbor dues on vessels of another nationality frequenting any port in such "sphere" than shall be levied on vessels of its own nationality, and no higher railroad charges over lines built, controlled, or

operated within its "sphere" on merchandise belonging to its citizens or subjects of other nationalities transported through such "sphere" than shall be levied on similar merchandise belonging to its own nationals transported over equal distances.

This specific request for certain limited economic rights constituted the original declaration of the Open Door policy. The phrase "spheres of influence" was placed in quotation marks, but Secretary Hay voiced no demand for their abolition. In the course of his entire note he made only one passing reference to Chinese sovereignty. That was not his primary concern. He merely sought some guarantee from the Powers that through their control over Chinese territory they would not seek to invalidate that right to most favored nation treatment which was incorporated in our treaties with the Chinese Government.

"We believe that 'a fair field and no favor' is all we require," Hay subsequently wrote in even simpler terms, "and with less than that we cannot be satisfied."

Little as the United States was asking, the European Powers did not welcome this note with any great enthusiasm. It implied a pledge of self-denial which would definitely restrict their commercial activities. It meant that any special privileges they forced the Chinese Government to extend to their nationals would be universal in application. But John Hay had placed them all in a difficult position. They had either to adhere to this declaration of policy or acknowledge their actual intention to discriminate against the nationals of other countries.

None of them quite dared to adopt such a candid attitude. Consequently they all accepted the American thesis. There was a general vagueness in some of their answers, and acceptance was made contingent upon that of the other Powers. The Russian reply was especially equivocal. But Hay wisely decided not to press for more definite assurances of good intentions, and he acted upon the assumption that the replies to his note constituted a complete acceptance of his program. On March 20, 1900, he formally announced to an expectant world that the assent of the Powers to his original proposal had been "final and conclusive."

Hay was immediately hailed as a world statesman for this achievement: he had settled the problem of the Far East. In this country press and pulpit acclaimed his service to peace and humanity.

"One of the most important diplomatic negotiations of our time," the *Journal of Commerce* stated, while the Chicago *Times Herald* declared more expansively that "there has never been a more brilliant and important achievement in diplomacy." The New York *Evening Post* characterized the exchange of notes as "a noble work of peace," and the Philadelphia *Press* proudly pointed out that this declaration of policy "protects the present, it safeguards the future, and it establishes the United States in an impregnable position."

In London, the *Times* politely appropriated for England the credit for formulating "that broad and just principle of international dealing in the Celestial empire," and then somewhat patronizingly gave the honor of winning international adherence "to our kinsmen across the Atlantic." The *Daily Mail* welcomed what it regarded as an American pledge "to take a leading part in the greatest task of the coming century, the reform of the Chinese Empire."

In one sense declaration of the Open Door policy, as formulated in 1900, amounted to very little. As a natural outgrowth of our traditional policy in the Far East, even though its announcement was largely inspired by Great Britain, it introduced no new principle into international relations in that part of the world. It merely constituted a reaffirmation of our right to most-favored-nation treatment in the commercial transactions of the Chinese Empire. Nor could the replies of the Powers to Secretary Hay's note be fully accepted as an inviolable pledge that they fully agreed to recognize and apply even this limited principle.

On the other hand, the declaration of the Open Door policy was of tremendous importance from two different angles: it aided in preventing any further developments at that time in the trend toward the final breakup of the Chinese Empire, and it gave to American foreign policy a new principle which was to win a place in public acceptance second only to that held by our precept against entangling alliances and the Monroe Doctrine.

In view of the more tangible influence of European rivalry in blocking the dismemberment of China, the latter aspect of the Open Door policy is possibly the more important. The commercial interests in this country accepted it as a pledge that the Government was committed to protect their trade and investments in China; liberal and religious interests interpreted it, although Hay had made no mention of national sov-

ereignty, as a promise that the United States undertook
to safeguard China's independence.

The religious interest in China, in fact, played an
important rôle in strengthening popular support for a
program which was primarily based on economic considerations. In 1900 there were about a thousand American missionaries in China representing some thirty societies, and through their activities there had developed,
at the close of the century, a widespread popular concern over the welfare of the Chinese. There was a universal desire that America should safeguard China's independence, and thereby permit the working out of
reforms in that country which reflected the impact of
American ideas.

This was in part an expression of national sympathy
for the under dog, the weak nation imposed upon by
stronger neighbors, and in part an expression of mis-
sionary zeal. It was the same spirit which led President
McKinley to declare that it was the duty of America
"to educate the Filipinos, and uplift and civilize and
Christianize them." It was the spirit of the chosen people going forth to spread among the heathen the beneficent light of American principles and American institutions.

Here was a strong force, its roots in the countless
church communities throughout the country which were
supporting the missions, building up American interest
in China. It was because of this popular feeling, as
much as through economic imperialism, that the Open
Door took its place as an integral feature of our Far
Eastern policy.

It has been ever since a symbol to which we have

faithfully clung, a symbol almost comparable to such other tokens of popular thought as "manifest destiny," or "national interest." It has been our adherence to the principles of the Open Door which has led us to obstruct Japan's expansion on the Asiatic mainland, when that country found the Open Door no longer in its interest, and to run all the risks such a policy involved. Public opinion has seldom stopped to analyze just what it might mean, or to evaluate the relative importance of those commercial and idealistic elements of which it is compounded.

CHAPTER III

THE BOXER REBELLION

AT THE TIME OF SECRETARY HAY'S ANNOUNCEMENT of the adherence of the Powers to his policy, occasional dispatches from the Far East were reporting sporadic outbreaks in the interior of China which appeared to be directed against foreigners. Secret societies known as the "Fists of Righteous Harmony," which the newspapers promptly translated as "Boxers," had gained a deep hold over the superstitious peasants. They were easily persuaded that all their troubles could be traced to the fearful machinations of the "foreign devils."

No one paid any great attention to these reports for a time. The ways of the Oriental were inscrutable; China was a strange and heathenish country. But no real fears were felt for the security of foreign lives and property. Nevertheless, the reverberations of the declaration of the Open Door policy had hardly died down before American troops were taking part in a foreign military expedition for the relief of the legations in Peking.

The Boxer uprising which sprang from the growing discontent aroused by foreign encroachments upon China was first largely directed against Chinese Christians. They were the traitors within the gates; they were also almost wholly defenseless. Bands of armed

37

peasants roamed the country-side, searching out the
Christians, robbing and slaying at will. As the disturbances spread, foreign lives were also endangered. Missionaries in the interior endeavoring to protect their
converts were seriously threatened.

On the Imperial Throne of China in this first year
of the new century, sat the Empress Dowager Tzu Hsi,
imperious, wilful, and imbued with a scornful hatred
of the foreigner which matched that of any Boxer.
Moreover, she was a shrewd and crafty ruler. She
realized that the Manchus themselves were foreigners,
and that the discontent of the peasantry might easily
be directed against the régime which she represented
as a Manchu overlord. Both policy and an instinct for
self-protection led her to sympathize with the Boxer
cause. And there were unquestionably times when the
Old Buddha, half convinced that there might be some
truth in the superstitious rigmarole whereby the Boxers
believed they could win immunity from foreign bullets,
saw visions of utilizing this antiforeign movement to
achieve her lifelong ambition of "driving the barba-
rians into the sea."

She did not dare support the Boxers openly. She knew
the hand of the foreigner was heavy. But she did not
hesitate to afford them secret encouragement. Her replies to the protests which the envoys of the Powers
promptly made, when foreign interests appeared to be
endangered, were politely evasive. Forced to issue de-
crees for the suppression of the mounting disorders, she
couched them in terms so ambiguous that none of her
officials could fail to understand that she was actually

warning them to proceed against the Boxers with the greatest circumspection.

As dispatches reporting these disturbances and the unsatisfactory attitude of the Imperial Court reached Washington, Secretary Hay refused to become alarmed. He instructed the American envoy in Peking to take such steps as appeared necessary to safeguard national rights, but he specifically pointed out that American policy in China had no other object than "to protect with energy American interests." Under these circumstances our minister was to act independently and to take part in any concurrent representations to the Chinese Government only in the case of absolute necessity. Above all, Secretary Hay declared, "there must be no alliances."

Events were to move too fast for Secretary Hay. The Boxers did not respect the niceties of international diplomacy. Secretly encouraged by the Empress Dowager, their forces gained strength. They began to converge upon Peking. An antiforeign movement had developed which was not only endangering property, but placing in jeopardy hundreds of lives. At last the envoys in the capital awoke to a very real and immediate crisis.

"Situation worse," the American minister cabled on June 4th. "It is possible we may be besieged in Pekin, with railroads and telegraphs cut. In that case I ask, as my colleagues are doing, that necessary instructions be given Admiral concert with other chiefs of squadron at Taku to take necessary measures warranted by the situation to eventually deliver Pekin."

A few days later he cabled again asking permission

to join with the other foreign envoys in demanding an imperial audience—"Answer quick."

"Yes," cabled Secretary Hay, and waited, anxious now, for the next dispatch.

None came.

For over a month a horror-stricken world daily expected news from the envoys they now knew to be besieged by the Boxers and, receiving none, became convinced that they had fallen victim to a murderous outburst. All hope was given up; a memorial service was planned in St. Paul's Cathedral in London. Then through devious channels and after long delay, a cipher message reached Washington.

"For one month we have been besieged in British legation under continual shot and shell from Chinese troops," reported the American minister. "Quick relief only can prevent general massacre."

Preparations were already under way for such relief, and foreign troops were being assembled at Tientsin. But doubts as to what was actually happening in Peking, the breakdown of communications, the general uncertainties characterizing the entire situation, the questions of international policy involved, all served to delay definite action. The world did not know whether it was about to war on China, or whether it was intervening only to protect the foreign envoys from the Boxers. The statesmen hesitated; national policies in the Far East were in the balance. But there was that graphic message—"Quick relief only can prevent general massacre."

Attempts to secure guarantees of safety for the beleaguered foreigners from the Imperial Government

brought little assurance. The Empress Dowager protested that intervention was unnecessary. It was proposed that any such move should be halted while the
foreigners were brought under official escort to Tientsin. But no confidence could be placed in a government which was known to be intriguing secretly with
the Boxer leaders and was taking no apparent measures
to drive them from the capital. To the suggestion that
the envoys leave the legations where they were defending themselves against shot and shell, the American
minister got a cable through stating bluntly that it
would mean "certain death."

Finally, on August 4th, a foreign relief expedition,
largely composed of Japanese and numbering in all
some nineteen thousand men, set out with the sole objective of reaching the capital in time. There was no
way of telling when the legations might be compelled
to surrender, or when the Imperial Government might
decide openly to throw its strength with the Boxers and
render further resistance futile.

As the foreign forces advanced, they met only slight
opposition. The Boxers were compelled to realize how
powerless they were against this determined display of
force. And in the meantime confusion mounted in the
Chinese capital. During those hot summer months when
the Boxers broke off their intermittent attacks on the
legations only to pillage and plunder throughout the
capital, Tzu Hsi wavered fearfully between an open attack on the foreigners and retreat from the vengeance
the relief force might administer. She listened first to
one adviser, then to another. She would first send sup-

plies to the legations and then urge the Boxers to destroy them.

Time sped on. She could not decide. The foreigners' fate hung on the whims of a wavering woman. But as they continued to hold out and the Boxers failed to make good their boasted promises, as the relief expedition gradually drew nearer and nearer Peking, Tzu Hsi at last took the action which saved the lives of the besieged envoys. She turned her back on the crisis and took refuge in sudden flight, secretly leaving the palace disguised as a peasant. The Imperial Court followed her in the utmost confusion; the Boxer leaders scattered to the four winds.

The relief expedition thereupon entered Peking, narrowly forestalling the disaster which for two months had been hanging over the heads of the 1,000 beleaguered foreigners and some 3,000 Chinese converts. Their casualties had risen to 76 killed and 179 wounded; none had escaped the privations and horrors of the siege.

The immediate task of the American Government, as that of the government of every other Power during the summer of 1900, had been the relief of the legations. Secretary Hay, however, did not forget the responsibilities the United States had newly assumed in the Far East through declaration of the Open Door policy. Through his notes to the Powers in 1899 he had sought to safeguard American interests, whatever action might be taken in regard to spheres of influence. In this new crisis, the Open Door in its broader sense was at once gravely threatened. The ultimate outcome of direct foreign intervention in China could hardly be foreseen.

Still uncertain of the fate of the envoys, completely ignorant of what was happening in Peking, Hay had taken an important step in support of his policy as early as July 3rd. He went further than he had in his earlier notes. He introduced the principle of respect for the political independence of China as a logical development of the idea of economic independence underlying the Open Door.

In a circular telegram, addressed to the governments of Germany, England, France, Russia, Japan, and the other nations taking part in the relief of the legations, he declared that the United States was determined to adhere to a policy of peace with China. While the Imperial Government would be held strictly accountable for any assaults upon American lives or property, the United States sought a solution of the crisis which would "bring about permanent safety and peace to China, preserve Chinese territorial and administrative entity, protect all rights guaranteed to friendly powers by treaty and international law, and safeguard for the world the principle of equal and impartial trade with all parts of the Chinese Empire."

America thus served notice upon the world that she would not seize upon the Boxer disorders as an excuse for acquiring new rights in China. We would throw the whole weight of our influence against any attempt on the part of the Powers to take advantage of China's helplessness. It was a practical, realistic move. Since there was no public support in the United States for acquiring further territory in the Far East—the Filipino insurrection had by now completely disillusioned the public as to the glories of territorial imperialism—Secretary Hay was determined to do what he could to make sure that no other nation secured any territory.

Moralistic interpretations of our policy as the disinterested friend of China were popular. Captain Mahan, whose persuasive pen was always at the service of naval and commercial expansion, found Divine guidance behind this stand to protect American markets. "The part offered us is great," he wrote in the *North American Review,* "the urgency is immediate, and the preparation made for us, rather than by us, in the unwilling acquisition of the Philippines, is so obvious as to embolden even the less presumptuous to see in it the hand of Providence."

Secretary Hay was more frank. Should a division of China be effected, the United States—in his own phrase —would be left out in the cold. Our influence in the Far East would be destroyed. It was "the devil's own mess," he confided in a letter to Whitelaw Reid, but he was determined "to hold on like grim death to the Open Door."

The real test for Secretary Hay, however, came not during the period of action but after the siege of the legations had been raised. His policy favored the negotiation of an agreement between the Powers and the Imperial Government which would provide adequate redress for the injuries inflicted upon the foreigners by the Boxers and guarantees for their future protection. At the same time it opposed the exaction of such terms as would seriously weaken the Imperial Government even if it did not alienate any of its territory.

The attitude of the other Powers did not augur too well for the success of his plans. If they could have agreed, the fate of China might well have been sealed. Germany took the position that there was no authentic Chinese Government with which the Powers could treat. She demanded the immediate execution of all the Boxer leaders. Russia gave every indication of planning to withdraw entirely from the concert of nations in order to reach a secret agreement with China which would assure her control of Manchuria. The other Powers appeared more anxious to obtain whatever concessions could be wrested from the impotent Imperial Government than to safeguard China's independence.

"There is, therefore, not a single power we can rely on," Secretary Hay wrote bitterly, "for our policy of abstention from plunder and the Open Door."

Moreover the Secretary of State discovered that the vagaries of American public opinion hardly served to strengthen his hand in the prospective negotiations. Strong pressure was being exerted for the immediate withdrawal of the American troops in China. Political opponents were raising the cry that the Administration was violating the Constitution by waging war on China without the authority of Congress. Hay felt that only the presence of a strong force in Peking could give to American policy the authority which would command the compliance of the Powers, and he had little patience with the idea that we could compel adherence to our doctrine on any other basis. "Mere flap-doodle" was his characterization of talk of "our preëminent moral position giving us the authority to dictate to the world."

While he was still in a position to do so, Hay consequently sent a strongly worded note to the representative of the Imperial Government with whom he had prevailed upon the Powers to deal. He stated emphatically that the United States was opposed to the conclusion of any individual agreement between China and any other nation. The note was also sent to all the interested Powers.

As in the case of the original Open Door notes, this communication placed the Powers in the position of either having to subscribe to the American policy or openly admit that it was their intention to wring further concessions from the Imperial Government. They had either to take their stand in favor of maintaining the concert of Powers in order to reach a fair and equitable adjustment of the quarrel with China, or publicly acknowledge that they had no intention of observing the principle behind the Open Door.

Confronted with this dilemma, they accepted Hay's leadership. They agreed to act in concert and respect China's sovereignty. As in her original stand upon the Open Door, however, the reply of Russia left something to be desired. Her note denied that the Russian Government had ever considered the negotiation of any secret agreement with China in regard to Manchuria, but in conclusion it ambiguously stated that in renouncing any special claims, the Imperial Russian Government would "quietly await the further march of events."

Some time before, President McKinley had used such a phrase in a significant statement. Justifying our own acquisition of the Philippines, he had declared that the "march of events rules and overrules human actions."

Whether or not the Imperial Russian Government was consciously echoing the sentiments of the American President, the expression had an ominous ring. Nor did Russia make any move toward withdrawing the troops she had dispatched to Manchuria for the supposed protection of foreign interests in the event of further Boxer disturbances.

Hay had no choice other than to accept the Russian disclaimer of territorial ambitions at its face value. He might privately declare that nation's vows to be "false as dicers' oaths when treachery is profitable," but such charges had no place in diplomatic correspondence. Again he proceeded on the theory that the Powers had not only subscribed to his policy, but had subscribed to it whole-heartedly.

Actual negotiations with the Chinese Government proceeded with heartbreaking delay. The American envoy in Peking followed a difficult path through the tortuous mazes of European diplomacy. Maintenance of a united front, and softening of the demands some of the Powers were determined to make upon China, called for a high measure of statesmanship. Even when the principle of a settlement which would ensure the continuance in power of the existing Chinese Government was agreed upon, the proposed indemnity for the losses sustained by the foreigners threatened to bankrupt the country.

No Power fully trusted any other. Each was accused of acting solely in its own interests. When public pressure finally forced the withdrawal of the American troops from Peking, we were charged with abandonment of our own stand in favor of the Open Door. It was said we were secretly acting in concert with Russia, solely because the Russian troops had also been withdrawn from the Chinese capital. It was a charge which rasped the frayed nerves of the State Department.

"If you break up a quiet whist party," Assistant Secretary Adee commented sarcastically, "by saying, 'Well, I'm going to bed, are you?' and I have to go, the game being spoiled, does it follow that I go home with you and get into your bed?"

There were separate negotiations between England and Germany which eventually resulted in a special agreement whereby the two countries specifically recognized each other's sphere of influence. It paid fulsome lip-service to the Open Door, and at first Hay hailed it joyfully as a further reaffirmation of his own policy. But a more significant feature was the exclusion of Manchuria from the scope of the understanding. No concerted action to safeguard the Open Door in its general application to all of China, the American Secretary of State was forced to realize, could be expected under prevailing international conditions. The Powers were still jockeying for special position in the Far East.

In so far as Japan was concerned, there continued to be strong support for the American policy on the straightforward grounds that it was serving to protect Japanese interests as effectively as those of the United States. While Japan would have been more than willing to accept any territory upon which she could get a grip in the event of China's partition, her hour had not yet come. Self-interest still dictated the closest coöperation with the United States in resisting any further European encroachments upon China.

In pursuing this program Japan had shown a marked willingness to subordinate any claims she might have against China to the general welfare. The only nation with a large force of troops readily available for the relief expedition, she had responded with alacrity to the requests of the other Powers for a Japanese contingent. Yet she had made no attempt to arrogate any special privileges for herself. It was, indeed, the first time Japan had participated on a basis of equality in an international expedition with European troops, and she was determined to demonstrate her right to be considered as an equal. During the occupation of Peking, her troops behaved with a forbearance which stood out in marked contrast to the attitude of certain of the European soldiery, and they won universal respect and admiration.

As events developed, moreover, Japan could not fail to see in Russian intrigues over Manchuria the handwriting on the wall. Whatever pledges Secretary Hay might elicit in favor of the Open Door, Tokyo realized that there was imminent danger of the establishment of a measure of Russian control in Northern China which would constitute a direct menace to her own national security. So real did this danger seem, in fact, that Japan would have liked to see the American policy strongly implemented. She would have welcomed assurances that in the event any nation violated the Open Door, there would be concerted action to enforce it.

With this end in view, Tokyo hopefully asked the United States what it would do, should Russia disregard her public pledges to adhere to the principles set

forth in the American notes respecting China's territorial integrity.

The Secretary of State had little to say. Hay was compelled to reply that "we were not at present prepared
singly, or in concert with other Powers, to enforce these
views in the East by any demonstration which could
present a character of hostility to any other Power."

Here was a first important statement of policy,
frankly recognizing that while America had taken the
lead in expounding the Open Door doctrine, she was not
prepared to adopt any active measures to uphold it. If
any nation was adamant in its refusal to observe China's
territorial integrity, Hay realized that popular support
for upholding it by force of arms was not forthcoming.

In protecting American interests in the Far East, he
could exert all the diplomatic influence at his command.
He could write all the notes he pleased insisting upon
maintenance of China's independence. But neither in
1901, nor at any time since, has public opinion in this
country given any mandate for military intervention.
Hay recognized this basic factor underlying the Open
Door policy; Theodore Roosevelt eventually accepted
it. Every time it has been ignored, and the United
States has found itself maneuvered into a position opposing some other Power prepared to use force, it has
had to retreat. The limitations as well as the possibilities of our Far Eastern policy had to be admitted almost
as soon as it was formulated.

Disregarding the reservations of Russia, Hay nevertheless succeeded, again with the important aid of European dissensions, in carrying his immediate program
through successfully. The terms of the protocol between

China and the Powers, finally signed on September 7, 1901, involved no territorial concessions and no special privileges for any Power. A huge indemnity, amounting to 450,000,000 Haekwan taels, was imposed upon the Imperial Government as retribution for the past; reservation of the Legation Quarter in Peking under foreign control, occupation of various points between Peking and the sea, and razing of the Chinese forts at Taku were demanded as guarantees for the future. China's territorial and administrative entity, however, remained intact.

The United States had reason to be satisfied with the part it had played in these negotiations.

"While we maintained complete independence," W. W. Rockhill stated in his final report as special envoy to China, "we were able to act harmoniously in the concert of powers, the existence of which was so essential to a prompt and peaceful settlement of the situation, we retained the friendship of all the negotiating powers, exerted a salutary influence in the cause of moderation, humanity and justice, secured adequate reparation for wrongs done our citizens, guarantees for their future protection, and labored successfully in the interests of the world in the cause of equal and impartial trade with all parts of the Chinese Empire."

A realistic appraisal of the situation would have compelled some modification of the roseate views held at the time as to the measure of success attained by Secretary Hay. No one of the Powers was actually committed to the Open Door policy whether in its narrower implications as embodied in the original Hay notes or in the broader interpretation comprising respect for China's territorial sovereignty. Their answers to the American notes had all been carefully reserved. And there were already signs that Russia felt herself in no way bound to respect Chinese independence.

Nevertheless, foreign intervention in China had not led to the expected division of the spoils. The empire had not been partitioned. Whatever the future might hold, China had been given a new lease on life.

Equally important from the American point of view, the doctrine of the Open Door and China's territorial integrity had become more deeply embedded than ever in the national consciousness. It had received its baptism by sword. We had taken our stand as the beneficent guardian of China; we were the defender of her independence. And involving as it did such a practical and also idealistic expression of the American spirit, the Open Door, for all our reluctance to maintain it by force, now commanded universal sanction as an integral phase of American foreign policy.

CHAPTER IV

THE RUSSO-JAPANESE WAR

IN THE YEARS IMMEDIATELY FOLLOWING THE BOXER Rebellion, American interest in Pacific affairs somewhat subsided. Establishment of the Open Door policy had not only been hailed as a great achievement; it had been interpreted as settling the problem of China. That country's division among the European Powers had been averted and American commercial interests appeared fully protected. For the public it was something of a relief to forget Far Eastern policy.

While the country was still a little intoxicated by its proud status as a new World Power, and the energetic Mr. Roosevelt was not only prepared but eager to dabble in international politics in any part of the world, the man in the street found interests nearer home more important. The Galveston tornado, gyrations of the New York Stock Exchange, the great anthracite coal strike of 1902, the seizure of Panama, bulked far larger in the public mind than anything happening on the other side of the Pacific.

For the State Department, custodian of a new foreign policy, the Far East could not be so easily forgotten. Representatives of those industrial interests for whose sake Secretary Hay had intervened in China were soon complaining that all was not well in Manchuria. It appeared that Russia was not carrying out her pledges to evacuate territory occupied during the Boxer Rebellion; that she was persistently trying to wring new concessions from the weak and ineffectual Chinese Government. In the process, American rights were being ignored. The Open Door, in short, was slowly swinging shut.

Washington dutifully protested, but its protests were either ignored or answered so evasively that the helpless officials of the State Department fumed in impotent rage. Seldom has the private correspondence of a President or a Secretary of State expressed such feelings of irritation against a foreign government as the letters of Roosevelt and Hay in their diatribes against Russia.

"Dealing with a government with whom mendacity is a science," wrote the Secretary of State on one occasion, "is an extremely difficult and delicate matter." The President fulminated against Russia's foreign policy, which he said was compounded of brutality, ignorance, arrogance, and short-sightedness. "Her diplomatists lied to us with brazen and contemptuous effrontery," Roosevelt declared, "and showed with cynical indifference their intention to organize China against our interests."

Count Cassini, the Russian Ambassador, possibly lacked something of the diplomatic finesse which might have been expected of an envoy of the Czar. While delivering his country's formal assurances of its faithful observance of all treaty engagements, he made little effort to hide his own opinion that Russia would never withdraw from Manchuria.

Secretary Hay intimated at one interview that if the Russian Government continued on its course, there would be nothing for the other Powers to do but take over certain other Chinese provinces. Count Cassini grew greatly excited.

"This is already done," he stormed. "China is dismembered, and we are entitled to our share."

Russia's basic policy was apparent. Regardless of any engagements entered into with the other Powers, or of any moral obligation to observe the Open Door, she was determined to establish unquestioned control over Manchuria. Imperialism was driving her to assert her position as a Pacific Power. And in reflection of the tortuous windings of continental diplomacy, both Germany and France were at the time encouraging her in an eastward expansion which diverted attention from other parts of the world where her ambitions might prove more troublesome.

The United States, as Hay had realized, could not offer any effective resistance to this Pacific advance. It was compelled to recognize Russia's "exceptional position" in northern China. But the Secretary of State sought by all the means at his command, as he wrote Roosevelt in May, 1902, to win assurances that "no matter what happens eventually in northern China and Manchuria, the United States shall not be placed in any worse position than while the country was under the unquestioned dominion of China."

To this end he insisted upon the opening up to foreign trade of two new Manchurian ports, Mukden and Antung, in the current negotiations with China for a new commercial treaty. The New York *Tribune* hailed this as a further victory for the Open Door. Hay himself knew better. Stronger measures were necessary to check

Russian encroachments and they were beyond his power. "I take it for granted," we find him writing despondently, "that Russia knows as we do that we will not fight over Manchuria, for the simple reason that we cannot. . . ."

Roosevelt was not yet ready to accept any such conclusion from declining popular interest in the Far East. He never did while Russia was the aggressor. As Hay drew back from any determined measures to implement his Open Door policy, the President grew more aggressive. "I have not the slightest objection," he told the Secretary of State, "to the Russians knowing that I feel thoroughly aroused and irritated at their conduct in Manchuria; that I don't intend to give way and that I am year by year growing more confident that this country would back me in going to an extreme in the matter."

By going to an extreme in the matter, did the forthright Mr. Roosevelt imply war? It was a strange aberration to believe that the American public was actually so concerned over the fate of Manchuria as to support a war against Russia. Hay sensed popular feeling far more accurately than the President. The country was not aroused over the issue; it hardly knew one existed.

Some thirty years later the situation was to be oddly paralleled. This time with Japan, and not Russia, in the rôle of the aggressor. Again the State Department was to protest, and again it was to find its protests unavailing. In 1932 as in 1902 there was no reason to believe that the public would uphold "going to an extreme in the matter." But the refusal of the United States to recognize any territorial adjustments resulting from

Japanese aggression in Manchuria reflected the persistence of the official view that vital American interests were involved.

While America took no active steps to uphold China's integrity by force of arms on either occasion, there was one country in the earlier period to which the status of Manchuria appeared a life and death matter. This was, of course, Japan. Her statesmen saw Russia, so largely instrumental in preventing Japan from asserting paramount power in Manchuria in 1894, blocking every opportunity for Japanese expansion on the Asiatic mainland. More than that, they saw the Slav, through control of Manchuria, pointing a dagger at the very heart of their country. Acquiescence in the Russian advance meant not only a death-blow to Japanese imperialism but an imminent threat to national safety. If the United States could afford to ignore this challenge to the Open Door, Japan was compelled to meet it.

In the determined stand now assumed, Tokyo looked for sympathy if not for actual support from both Great Britain and the United States. In the case of the former nation it was definitely assured through the Anglo-Japanese Alliance. This treaty had been concluded in 1902, as a consequence of British fears of Russian aggression. The two nations had agreed that in the event of one becoming engaged in war, the other should remain neutral unless another Power intervened. In that case it would come to its ally's aid. The United States had made no such commitments. Our professed interest in blocking the Russian advance in Manchuria and in upholding the Open Door nevertheless could be counted upon to make us almost a silent partner in the Anglo-Japanese Alliance.

There was little realization at this time that the possible consequences of a Russo-Japanese war over Manchuria might be the substitution of Japanese aggression for Russian aggression. Although Japan had already shown that she felt she had a primary interest in Manchuria, her support of the Open Door policy and ready acceptance of the principle that China's integrity should be preserved had led to the belief that she would continue to coöperate in application of the Hay doctrines. Russia was so distinctly the villain of the piece that public opinion in this country readily fell in line with the Rooseveltian belief that what the Japanese sought in Manchuria "was what all civilized Powers in the East were contending for."

In any event, Japan presented Russia with an ultimatum which in effect demanded a reaffirmation of her pledge to maintain Chinese sovereignty in Manchuria. Russia refused to make any such commitment. Japan summarily declared war.

In conformity with the policy of the other Powers, the United States announced its neutrality. Unofficially, however, President Roosevelt, now personally directing foreign policy due to the illness of Secretary Hay, took an unprecedented step which gave concrete expression to his sympathy with the Japanese cause. He was not a man to follow any half-hearted, lukewarm policy. Firm in his conviction that American interests were deeply involved in the possible fate of Manchuria, and that Japan was the more ready to respect them than Russia, he took it upon himself to forestall any outside intervention which might prejudice Japan's chance of victory in this critical struggle.

"As soon as this war broke out," he wrote Cecil Spring-Rice on July 24, 1905, "I notified Germany and France in the most polite and discreet fashion that in the event of a combination against Japan to try to do what Russia, Germany and France did to her in 1894, I should promptly side with Japan and proceed to whatever length was necessary on her behalf. I of course knew that your government would act in the same way, and I thought it best that I should have no consultation with your people before announcing my own purpose."

Two questions are immediately posed: Was any such threat of intervention necessary? Would the American people have supported intervention if events had forced Roosevelt to attempt to carry out his threat?

It can only be said that at no time did Germany or France give any indication of extending effective support to Russia, and that in view of the terms of the Anglo-Japanese Alliance, it was extremely unlikely that they would have considered doing so. Nor is there the slightest evidence that the American people would have allowed their country to be plunged into a world war on no other ground than defense of Japan's interests in Manchuria as a means of upholding the Open Door.

Roosevelt had, of course, no warrant for pledging American intervention under any circumstances. But while the Constitution entrusts the war-making power to Congress, it is the prerogative of the Executive to create a situation for which no other solution than war is sometimes possible. Roosevelt was running a risk which his ignorance of the stakes of European diplomacy did not allow him properly to evaluate.

What might have happened had France or Germany actually attempted to prevent Japan from achieving her war aims must be an open question. Roosevelt himself apparently believed, in retrospect, that his discreet hints aided in localizing a conflict which might otherwise have ushered in the World War ten years earlier than it actually broke out. A good many years later he was to intimate that if President Wilson had taken a similar stand in regard to Belgian neutrality, a world war would again have been averted.

Along less spectacular lines, the United States also made at this time a direct move to safeguard the independence of China, and therefore our own commercial opportunities in the Far East. Secretary Hay officially sought a declaration from the neutral Powers that, whatever the consequences of the Russo-Japanese War, they would not seek from China any concessions of territory or special privileges incompatible with the principle of the Open Door. Again the replies to the American note were favorable and our leadership in safeguarding China further confirmed.

In the meantime the war between Japan and Russia proceeded without undue regard for the diplomatic entanglements which the other Powers were weaving about it. Again to the astonishment of the Western World, whose admiration and sympathy for Japan were touched with a complacent sense of superiority, the little island kingdom began to win a succession of spectacular victories. On both land and sea, the Japanese forces proved themselves more than a match for those of Russia.

An attack had been launched on the Russian fleet off Port Arthur immediately after war had been declared, in February, 1904, and after a short engagement the enemy ships had limped back to port badly crippled. It was a strategic if not a decisive victory, clearly proving Japanese naval superiority, and the Russian fleet thereafter remained bottled up at Port Arthur. But even more decisive in the history of the Far East was the first land engagement, the battle of the Yalu. It was a spectacular victory for Japanese arms, spectacular because the Russians were clearly beaten on the field and the illusion once and for all shattered that the Japanese could not stand up against white troops.

A further Japanese victory was won at the battle of Nanshan, as a prelude to the succession of furious assaults on Port Arthur which were eventually to lead to its capitulation, and the main Russian forces fell back toward Liao-yang. Again the Japanese attacked and again inflicted a severe defeat. This time their forces were inferior to those of the Russians, and an admiring world could not fail to recognize the gallantry of this new-comer on the international stage.

The battle of Liao-yang had taken place in August and for the next six months, while the siege of Port Arthur continued, the main armies of the two nations were engaged in preparations for what was realized would be the final test of their strength. Port Arthur finally fell on January 2, 1905, but on land the deadlock continued, a test of endurance in which Japan was undergoing a crippling drain of men and money, and

Russia combatted not only the serious difficulties involved in the transportation of men and supplies from Europe but a growing popular discontent with the war.

The battle of Mukden was fought in March with 300,000 troops engaged on each side, and the issue was not long in doubt. The Russians could not stand up against the Japanese attack; the latter's victory was decisive. The collapse of the Czar's power in the Far East could no longer be doubted.

One possible threat remained. The Russians had dispatched their Baltic fleet to the Far East, and should it succeed in defeating that of Japan, they would regain command of the sea. But in the battle of Tsushima, on May 27, 1905, the entire fleet, on which Russia's hopes for revenging her previous defeats had rested, was either captured or sunk.

These unexpected and dramatic developments created a deep concern, both in Washington and in the European capitals, as to the possible consequences of the war. While Roosevelt had both hoped for and expected a Japanese victory, he had not anticipated quite so smashing a triumph as that which Japan appeared to be winning. On the day of Port Arthur's surrender, as Secretary Hay confided to his diary, the President was still convinced that the United States should not "permit Japan to be robbed a second time of the fruits of her victory," but he was beginning to foresee the possibility of a too-powerful Japan seriously upsetting the balance of power in the Far East.

Roosevelt continued to have great admiration for Japan. The efficiency, the martial spirit, the ambitious pride of her people appealed greatly to him. He made no pretense of concealing his feeling and enthusiastically studied everything he could about the country. He even adopted jiu-jutsu as a part of his program of the strenuous life. But he wondered about the future.

"I wish I were certain," he wrote about this time, "that the Japanese down at bottom did not lump Russians, English, Americans, Germans, all of us, simply as white devils inferior to themselves not only in what they regard as the essentials of civilization, but in courage and forethought, to be politely treated only so long as would enable the Japanese to take advantage of our various national jealousies, and beat us in turn."

The President thus became anxious for an end to hostilities. And he saw in this situation an opportunity for the United States, and also for himself, not only to promote the cause of world peace but to win new international prestige.

In the subsequent negotiations which eventually enabled Roosevelt to bring Japan and Russia together at the conference table, the President's unexpected ally was the German Kaiser. Their association constitutes a strange chapter in diplomacy. Each had a very definite admiration for the other. The Kaiser considered Roosevelt one of the few statesmen who really understood him. As he wrote the Russian Czar on one occasion, "we are very intimate with each other." And while Roosevelt scoffed at the idea that he would really follow the lead of "a man who is so jumpy, so little capable of continuity of action, and therefore, so little capable of being loyal to his friends or steadfastly hostile to his enemies," he was at times very much under the Kaiser's influence.

He never fully understood just what Wilhelm's motives were during the period of the Russo-Japanese War. Even if he had been better informed than he actually was, it would have been extremely difficult to follow the thread of the Kaiser's erratic diplomacy. His changing policy in the Far East was in fact but a phase of the frantic efforts Germany was making to break through the encircling wall of alliances which England, France, and Russia were slowly building about her. They led the ambitious Kaiser, during these hectic years which were an ominous prelude to the catastrophe of 1914, to attempt to detach Russia from France, to seek out the coöperation of Great Britain, and assiduously to cultivate the friendship of the United States. In the Far East he successively encouraged Russia in an aggressive policy in regard to Manchuria, took a strong stand in favor of the Open Door, and finally exercised all his influence to bring the Russo-Japanese War to a close.

Roosevelt's first efforts to elicit the Kaiser's support in favor of peace awoke no response, and in regard to one such proposal the latter's stand was certainly the more realistic. For the President made the suggestion that Manchuria should be neutralized, with the appointment by Germany of a Chinese viceroy to exercise a nominal Chinese sovereignty. The Kaiser thought the idea "simply nonsense," and shrewdly noted in the margin of the dispatch: "One must not divide the hide of the bear before he has been shot."

More definite overtures by Roosevelt in February, 1905, when intimations had reached him that Japan was really becoming interested in the possibilities of peace, were also hastily dismissed by his German friend.

This move the Kaiser characterized as "quite a rash and none too tactful act . . . pregnant with dangerous consequences."

He was not ready for peace. He would have liked to see Russia further embroiled in the Far East. His own scheme for a Russo-German defensive alliance having collapsed, he wished to see the Czar weakened as much as possible. It was only when the outbreak of revolution in Russia raised the specter of the collapse of the Empire and the possible spread of antimonarchist agitation across the German border, that he was ready to throw his influence for peace into the international scales.

Roosevelt in the meantime was moving cautiously. But after the battle of Tsushima—an action in which Admiral Togo flew the signal: "The destiny of the Empire depends upon this one battle"—the Japanese Government definitely sought his good offices. It proposed that after sounding out the situation, Roosevelt should invite the two belligerents, on his own initiative, to discuss possible terms of peace. Here was the opportunity for which the President had been waiting. His first task was to discover informally whether the Russian Government would welcome such a move before he approached it directly.

To that end he sought the help of Germany, and the Kaiser now obligingly wrote the Czar of the importance of bringing hostilities to a close as speedily as possible. He pointed out the great influence which America exercised in Japan, and the advantage of securing the mediation of President Roosevelt. He would be glad, Wilhelm told the Czar, to get privately in touch with Roosevelt and suggest that he make a definite move to bring about peace if the Russian Government should approve.

The Czar was reluctant to abandon the war. Russia had far greater reserves and was confident of her ability to crush the upstart empire which had inflicted such disastrous defeats upon her army and navy. But revolution was threatening at home. He told the Kaiser that peace negotiations might be feasible.

When the American Ambassador sought an audience in St. Petersburg, he consequently found the Czar ready to accede to Roosevelt's suggestion. "You have come at a psychological moment," Nicholas told him. "As yet no foot has been placed on Russian soil; but I realize that at any moment they can make an attack upon Sakhalin. Therefore it is important that the meeting should take place before that occurs."

With assurances that neither of the belligerents would reject his overtures, Roosevelt then proposed a peace conference. Japan and Russia both agreed. After some preliminary negotiations, Washington was accepted as a neutral site, later changed to Portsmouth, New Hampshire, as more suitable in the August heat.

Roosevelt had been acting entirely in behalf of Japan throughout these negotiations, clearly recognizing that despite her victories she could not maintain a prolonged struggle against an enemy with far superior resources, but he had no doubt that he was acting not only in the interests of peace but in the best interests of the United States. Japan's general war aims were fully approved. The complete withdrawal of Russia from Korea and the acquisition of Russian rights in South Manchuria were the fruits of victory which Roosevelt had been prepared to assure Tokyo even at the cost of intervention.

Moreover, Japan had repeatedly stated that Manchuria would be returned to China and that she had no intention of holding any Chinese territory. She had reiterated her determination to uphold the Open Door. The original Anglo-Japanese Alliance bore witness to the two Powers' special interest "in maintaining the independence and territorial integrity of China and the Empire of Korea. . . ." When the alliance was renewed in 1905, during the course of the war, any mention of Korea was expressly omitted. Nevertheless, "the preservation of the common interests of all the Powers in China by insuring the independence and integrity of the Chinese Empire" was again one of its major provisions.

Roosevelt realized that Japan was not actuated by any altruistic motives, and he had become somewhat fearful of the consequences of her winning too great power, but he still believed that "on the mainland in China her policy is the policy to which we are already committed." Peace at this particular stage represented a peace which, it was believed, would most effectively strengthen America's position in the Orient and safeguard her opportunities for trade and commerce.

With Japan's military and naval supremacy beyond question, Russia had no ground for resisting the major Japanese demands. The negotiations at Portsmouth proceeded smoothly enough to a certain point. Russia agreed to recognize Japan's special position in Korea and to surrender all Russian rights and privileges in South Manchuria. A crisis developed, however, over the further demand of Japan for cession of Sakhalin and payment of an indemnity. Here Russia, feeling she was being pushed too far, refused to make further concessions. Her plenipotentiaries were instructed to break off negotiations if a satisfactory agreement was not reached on these points.

Roosevelt had not heretofore intervened in the negotiations. Now he felt compelled to exert whatever pressure was at his command upon both governments. He solemnly appealed to them "in the name of all that is lofty and noble" not to let this opportunity to end the war escape. He also again called upon the Kaiser to use his influence with the Czar.

As the final session of the peace conference opened, the issue was very much in doubt. Very solemnly the Russian envoy, the popular Count Witte, handed a note to the head of the Japanese delegation. Baron Komura. In it Russia categorically refused to pay any indemnity, but agreed to cede the southern half of Sakhalin.

"Absolute silence reigned for a few seconds," reads the account of an eye-witness. "Witte, as usual, kept tearing up the paper that was lying beside him. . . . The Japanese continued to be enigmatic.

"At last Komura, in a well-controlled voice, said that the Japanese Government, having for its aim the restoration of peace and the bringing of the negotiations to a successful conclusion, expressed its consent to Russia's proposal to divide Sakhalin in two, without indemnity being paid. Witte calmly replied that the Japanese proposal was accepted and that the line of demarcation would be reckoned the fiftieth degree."

PRESIDENT THEODORE ROOSEVELT AND THE
ENVOYS TO THE PORTSMOUTH CONFERENCE
Left to right: Count Witte, Baron Rosen, President Roosevelt,
Baron Komura, Baron Takahira.

In this fashion the Treaty of Portsmouth was agreed upon. Japan had fallen heir to Russia's position in South Manchuria. No Power intervened. Throughout the world, President Roosevelt was hailed for his contribution to the peace of the Far East and the peace of the world.

CHAPTER V

SEEDS OF CONTROVERSY

Public opinion in the united states had heartily upheld the policy of benevolent neutrality toward Japan during her war with Russia. While it is incredible that the possible intervention in that conflict contemplated by President Roosevelt could have commanded any popular support, an interest in things Japanese and an enthusiasm for the exploits of the Japanese army and navy swept the country. Their every victory was applauded in the press with a fervor which could hardly have been less neutral in feeling.

The various reasons for American sympathy for Japan had wide appeal. She was the smaller nation fighting for her life. She was defending China, our traditional ward, against an aggressive and barbaric foe. She was waging war against the corruption and treachery of the Slav in behalf of other nations as well as in her own behalf. She stood as the champion of commercial rights in the Far East. While the war could hardly be called one to make the world safe for democracy, it was vaguely considered as one to make the world safe from Russian autocracy.

Evidence of this popular attitude was everywhere apparent. The press had nothing but praise for Japan; it poured scorn and ridicule on Russia. It was repeatedly pointed out that the Russian policy in Manchuria was

a direct menace to American interests, while a possible
Japanese ascendancy in Eastern Asia was welcomed as
a guarantee for the protection of our rights.

This attitude, not unsurprisingly, was bitterly resented in Russia. The press was given free rein to condemn what the Russian Government regarded as America's betrayal of Western solidarity against the Orient.
Japan's real strength "lies in the support of the United
States," declared the official organ at Port Arthur. From
St. Petersburg came reports that Japan was being made
the cat's-paw for carrying out "the well-known policy
of President Roosevelt, who has repeatedly claimed
that the Pacific Ocean, with all its islands and coasts, is
the proper sphere of American domination."

With Count Cassini angrily protesting in Washington
and the State Department finding it more and more
difficult to maintain that America was really neutral,
relations between the two countries were seriously
strained. European opinion appeared convinced that
war was a distinct possibility.

As the course of the Russo-Japanese conflict pointed
more clearly to a victory for Japan, however, the first
signs began to appear of what was going to be one of
the most remarkable transformations of public opinion
which has ever occurred in this country. Japan was winning her battles too easily; her triumph seemed to be
too complete. The horrid doubt which had already occurred to Mr. Roosevelt sprang up in the popular mind:
a Japan fortified by so spectacular a defeat of Russia
might not prove to be as self-denying a friend of peace
in the Far East as had originally been expected. It was

belatedly recognized that Japan might place her own interests in the Orient above those of the West.

Something of a sensation was caused by a report in the New York *Herald* of the changed psychology of the Japanese since their victories over the Russians. They had become "insufferably overbearing and insolent," wrote a correspondent from Japan, and appeared to have lost all respect for the superior virtues of the White Race. They were casting covetous eyes on the Philippines. "In the navy it is generally believed," this observer further stated, "that we will have to meet Japan's fleets on the Pacific before the century is old."

This was an ominous note. It represented a distinct change from the conception of the noble little Japs fighting the battle of civilization. Still, faith was strong. "Better a Japan dominating Asia than a Russia, a Germany, an England, or an America," declared the Springfield *Republican*. "Japan in the opinion of many of our population," the Kansas City *Journal* stoutly reiterated, "is fighting America's battles as well as her own." The *Literary Digest* continued to carry advertisements of correspondence courses in jiu-jutsu.

During the peace negotiations, however, new impetus was given to the anti-Japanese shift in public opinion. In part this was due to the skilful propaganda of the Russian envoys who spared no effort to win back American sympathy for the humbled colossus of the North; in part it was due to the arrogant and self-assured bearing of the Japanese envoys. But beneath these immediate causes was the now inevitable realization that a Japan which was supplanting Russia in South Manchuria and clearly planning to annex Korea, had become a World

Power. In any possible conflict of interests, she could no longer be expected to accede quietly to whatever policy the United States might promulgate.

At the same time opinion in Japan, which had been enthusiastic for America as an unofficial ally in the struggle against Russia, awoke to the possibility that the United States might stand athwart the path of future Japanese expansion in the Western Pacific. The intervention of President Roosevelt in the peace negotiations was popularly interpreted as an attempt to deprive Japan of the full reward of her victory over Russia. The loss of the indemnity was bitterly resented. As the press in this country began to question the motives of Japanese policy in Manchuria, cables from the Far East told of anti-American riots in Tokyo.

After half a century of friendship and confidence, an element of distrust and suspicion had definitely entered into American-Japanese relations. Each nation had sensed in the other a potential rival. In subsequent years there were to be periods when this distrust became so pronounced that controversies which otherwise could have been easily settled awoke talk of war. There were also to be periods when America and Japan were able to work out their problems in close coöperation. But the close of the Russo-Japanese War marked a definite turning-point in the attitude of the two nations toward each other. They could never again recapture the mutual confidence which had previously characterized their relations.

The logic of this situation was inescapable. Whatever ambitions Japan had had before 1904, she was powerless to pursue them. But the defeat of Russia left her free to

expand her power in Eastern Asia. In so far as the
United States hoped to make American influence a
dominating factor in the development of China, it now
had to face the rivalry of a strong Power whose interests
on the Asiatic mainland were more immediate and more
vital. The stage was set for a new struggle over the
Open Door and Chinese independence. A new epoch
had opened in the history of the Pacific.

Nor was it long before there was concrete evidence
of the divergence of Japanese and American interests
in the Far East. Our position had been predicated on
the theory that the two nations were mutually pledged
to observe the Open Door and to protect China. Japan's
repeated assurances on this vital point had been taken
at their face value. But the United States had no more
than adjusted itself to the fact that Japan was taking
over Russian interests in South Manchuria than the
State Department was receiving complaints from American business men in the Far East. Their trade was
being more hampered by the Japanese authorities than
it ever had been by the Russians.

The State Department took up the problem cautiously. In a soft-spoken, diplomatic note it expressly
recognized the well-known purpose of the Japanese
Government to maintain absolute equality of trade in
Manchuria, and merely intimated, in the most polite
terms, "that unauthorized subordinates may be failing
to execute the purposes of the Government of Japan."

Tokyo replied in terms no less circumspect. Its note
gently suggested that this indeed must be the case if
there actually was any discrimination against American

trade. For the Government had decided that the Open Door policy should be vigorously enforced.

Here the matter was allowed to rest. Japan had inaugurated her policy of self-righteously keeping the door to trade in Manchuria open in principle, and carefully closing it in practice.

Against the background of this basic change in the relationship between Japan and the United States, a more immediate controversy sprang up in 1906. It did not involve any fundamental question of foreign policy. But it was inextricably entwined with those imponderables of national dignity and national honor which Japan was now more than ever eager to defend because of her new position in the Far East.

For some time there had been on the West Coast, and especially in California, a strong anti-Japanese feeling which arose not out of any developments in Asia but from the immigration problem. Since 1900 there had been a steady influx of Japanese coolie labor. Various labor and political groups in California had sensationally magnified this movement into a menace to American institutions and to the American standard of living. It mattered little that the actual number of Japanese immigrants was too small to merit one-tenth the alarm their presence caused. Newspaper sensationalism and political agitation had created a burning issue.

"The feeling on the Pacific slope . . . is as foolish as if conceived by the mind of a Hottentot," Roosevelt wrote Lodge. Nevertheless, the feeling existed. It was bound to cause trouble.

This trouble developed when the San Francisco

school-board bowed before the current wave of anti-Japanese hysteria by decreeing that all children of Oriental parentage should be barred from the regular schools and segregated in a special institution. Not many children were involved. But the order constituted an act of flagrant discrimination very definitely directed against the Japanese.

The protest from Japan was immediate and vehement, and even more emphatic than this official note was the reaction of Japanese public opinion. The United States was widely attacked for what was interpreted as an open and entirely unwarranted insult to the national honor. The press demanded immediate revocation of the school-board's ruling and redress for the injury done Japanese pride.

In turn, California's reaction to the feeling aroused in Japan was an inevitable flare-up of even more intense anti-Japanese sentiment. The whole immigration issue was thrown into the boiling cauldron of racial prejudice. While on the Atlantic seaboard the controversy was considered a tempest in a teapot, the West became more and more violent in its demand for action against the Japanese immigrants.

From Japan came talk of possible war. One conservative Tokyo paper declared that "even traditional friendship will not escape a rupture should incidents like those which have occurred in San Francisco be repeated." "Should diplomacy fail to bring about a proper solution," stated another, "the only way open to us is an appeal to arms."

There is no evidence that responsible authorities in Tokyo had any idea of challenging America on the immigration issue, but Japan was in a self-confident, belligerent mood as a result of her victories over Russia. Roosevelt thought war possible. "The Japanese," he wrote, "are proud, sensitive, warlike, and flushed with the glory of their recent triumph, and are in my opinion bent upon establishing themselves as the leading power in the Pacific."

Under these circumstances, and convinced that the action of the San Francisco school-board was "a wicked absurdity . . . a crime against a friendly nation," his policy had a threefold objective: to convince Japan that sentiment in California in no sense reflected the feeling of this country as a whole, to compel the San Francisco school-board to withdraw its segregation order, and to reach an equitable solution of the whole immigration problem.

His action on the first of these points was the dispatch of a firm but conciliatory reply to the Japanese protest; on the second, direct intervention with the San Francisco authorities ultimately resulted in the cancellation of the segregation order. The immigration problem was more difficult. It was at least temporarily settled, however, by an informal understanding with the Japanese Government, concluded in February, 1908. Through this so-called Gentlemen's Agreement, Japan undertook herself to withhold passports from coolie labor attempting to enter the United States.

Roosevelt's attitude during this period shows him in an unusual light. The sometime truculent, belligerent President was unexpectedly conciliatory and pacific. It was an attitude springing from two causes: his conviction that in this particular controversy the United States was completely in the wrong because of the unwarranted anti-Japanese agitation in California, and his belief that in the aftermath of a successful war, public opinion in Japan might actually force the Government over its own better judgment to take up arms in defense of national honor.

Through his moderate policy, in any event, the martial Mr. Roosevelt laid himself open for a time to accusations of truckling to Japan. "Tiddy Rosenfelt," at a time when war rumors were flying about thickly, was pictured by the ineffable Mr. Dooley as hiding under his bed, "with a small language book trying to say 'Spare us' in the Japanese tongue."

It was not an entirely justified reproach. Roosevelt could not long act so out of character, and he was always a big navy advocate. Despite his attitude of conciliation, he was prepared to stand up for our rights should Japan carry her protests too far, and to maintain at all costs that political supremacy in the Pacific which he considered America's destiny. He strongly favored, as he wrote Senator Hale during this immigration controversy, "keeping our navy in such shape as to make it a risky thing for Japan to go to war with us."

When, indeed, prior to conclusion of the Gentlemen's Agreement, Japan appeared to show little disposition to accept his friendly overtures in the spirit in which they were made, he decided upon a peculiarly Rooseveltian gesture. He would send the fleet to the Pacific. It was a move decided upon not as a threat, but as an uncompromising exhibition of American naval strength. It was intended to convince the militaristic elements in Japan, once and for all, that their country could not afford to pick a quarrel with the United States.

The proposed dispatch of the fleet to the Pacific represented, in 1907, a hazardous and courageous undertaking whose significance today can hardly be appreciated. No other Power had ever attempted maneuvers on such a grand scale. It was hardly believed possible that the fleet could make the long voyage about Cape Horn—for the Panama Canal was not yet built—without gravely impairing its effectiveness as a fighting unit. And whatever happened, the Atlantic Coast would be left defenseless until the fleet returned.

Roosevelt, nevertheless, took this significant step completely on his own initiative, and, in retrospect at least, he attributed it entirely to his determination to impress Japan.

"I had been doing my best to be polite to the Japanese," he wrote some years later, "and had finally become conscious of a very, very slight undertone of veiled truculence in their communications in connection with things that happened on the Pacific slope; and I finally made up my mind that they thought I was afraid of them. . . . I definitely came to the conclusion . . . it was time for a showdown."

The announcement that the fleet was going to the Pacific created an immediate and violent outbreak of controversy. It inevitably intensified the war rumors which had now been flying about for over a year. Opinion in this country was sharply divided on whether it was a move likely to bring Japan to a more sober realization of the dangers of the situation, or whether it might not provoke actual hostilities.

All during the summer of 1907 the storm raged. The naval maneuvers were attacked as an unwarranted threat directed against a nation with whom the United States was at peace. They were held to be absolutely necessary; they were decried as utterly useless. The pacifists shrieked in alarm; the jingoes preached preparedness. The West hailed this demonstration of American firmness, and the East trembled at its possible consequences. In a double-leaded editorial, the New York *Sun* solemnly stated: "The navy is going to the Pacific Ocean for the war with Japan."

Roosevelt nevertheless went ahead with his plans, on the one hand assuring the Japanese that his intentions were entirely peaceful, and on the other making certain that the fleet was prepared for all eventualities, Secretary Taft, stopping off at Tokyo on his way home from a visit to the Philippines, took occasion to declare that "under the circumstances nothing is more infamous than the suggestion of war."

The fleet—sixteen battle-ships strong—rounded Cape Horn without experiencing any of those disasters which had been so fearfully predicted and in March, 1908, carried out its maneuvers off the California Coast. The further announcement was then made that the voyage would be continued around the world.

In the meantime the threat of war had quietly died away; the excitement had subsided. Japan had met our protests in regard to immigration by conclusion of the Gentlemen's Agreement. There was nothing left for the war jingo, an editorial in the New York *Mail* stated, "but to close his marionette show and pack up his puppets in moth balls."

Roosevelt attributed this change in the international atmosphere entirely to our display of naval strength. "Every particle of trouble with the Japanese Government and the Japanese press," he later wrote, "stopped like magic as soon as they found that our fleet had actually sailed, and was obviously in good trim." In his opinion it had demonstrated not only to Japan but to all the world that the United States had acted with fairness throughout the controversy *"and that we carry a big stick."*

How really serious were the dangers Roosevelt conjured up, and how much he allowed himself to be swept away by the hysteria on the Pacific Coast, are moot points. It was at least fortunate that he did not allow his fears of war to foster a more belligerent attitude. For the situation was at best ticklish, and the opinion has prevailed in many quarters that the United States actually came closer to war with Japan at this time than it ever has since.

In an article which appeared in the magazine *Asia,* in July, 1923, this statement was made: "Outside the executive departments at Washington it has never been known in this country that, during the nervous days in the early summer of 1908, the United States hovered on the edge of an ultimatum from Japan." Its author bore the same surname, and was subsequently to hold the same post, as the President in this period. Whatever the truth of the story, it indicates a point of view which Franklin Delano Roosevelt probably gained while in the Navy Department.

The dénouement, in any event, was now a happy one. Japan formally invited the fleet to call at Tokyo on its around-the-world voyage and the invitation was cordially accepted.

In startling contrast to the reports emanating from Tokyo a year earlier, the cables from the Far East were soon telling of the enthusiastic reception which the Japanese had accorded the American sailors. As they went ashore in Tokyo they were greeted by ten thousand school children happily singing *Hail Columbia, Happy Land*. Aboard our flag-ship, visiting Japanese naval officers carried the American ambassador about the deck on their shoulders amid the crew's enthusiastic cheers.

Coincident with these favorable developments in American-Japanese relations, negotiations were also proceeding in regard to the more basic issues involved in the two nations' respective positions in the Far East. As early as July, 1905, in fact, Roosevelt had reached an unofficial understanding with Japan which constituted a frank recognition of certain of the changes in that part of the world resulting from the Russo-Japanese War. In return for assurance from the Tokyo Government that it had no designs against the Philippines, he promised a policy of coöperation in regard to relations with China and virtually recognized the validity of a Japanese protectorate over Korea.

Consequently no protest had been voiced by the United States when Japan proceeded, despite her previous engagements to respect Korean independence, to incorporate Korea as an integral part of the Japanese Empire. In the conviction that this helpless country had neither the ability to maintain an independent government nor the right to expect any foreign intervention in its behalf, no obstacle was placed in the path of Japan's first concrete move to extend her empire to the Asiatic mainland.

This development was not held to affect in any way the principle of the Open Door. America still believed Japan intended to uphold this principle in China and was perfectly willing to close her eyes to any possible lesson to be learned from Tokyo's flagrant violation of previous pledges in regard to Korea. But in consequence of the friction which had developed over other matters, and the inescapable evidence of a new attitude of distrust in Japanese-American relations which could not be entirely dispelled by ten thousand school children singing *Hail Columbia, Happy Land,* it seemed auspicious, in 1908, to reaffirm the common policy of the two Powers toward China.

The initiative for this move came from Japan. She was concerned over current negotiations between the Chinese and certain American financiers in regard to railroad construction in Manchuria, and sought assurances that the United States would not interfere with her own plans. In addition to the two nations reasserting their intention to respect each other's territorial possessions and to support the integrity of China, what has since been known as the Root-Takahira Agreement consequently went considerably further in regard to Manchuria.

"The policy of both governments, uninfluenced by any aggressive tendencies," this agreement stated, "is directed to the maintenance of the existing *status quo* in the region above mentioned."

So far had Roosevelt advanced along the road toward recognition of Japan's special position in Manchuria. It was not as conclusive an acceptance of this position as was subsequently to be sought by Japan, but it marked the President's realistic acquiescence in her supplanting of Russian influence in South Manchuria. America would not interfere. We accepted the status quo even though American business interests were at this very time querulously complaining that it meant the closing of the Open Door.

Roosevelt's policy had thus swung around a broad circle. He had resented Russian encroachments upon China—declaring that he was not averse to having St. Petersburg know that we were prepared, if necessary, to go to "an extreme in the matter"—but now he was ready to recognize that Japan had special interests in Manchuria whose frank acceptance was the only practical policy for this country to follow. This was in part due to his temperamental admiration for the Japanese in contrast to his suspicions of Russia. He also saw that Japan could not be restrained, short of war, from an expansion on the Asiatic mainland which was a natural concomitant of her national growth.

Roosevelt at times wandered far afield in his Far Eastern policy. When the aggressor was Russia, he had been apparently willing to make commitments for which he had little warrant. But in the end he reached firm ground. Few American statesmen have at one and the same time had as keen a sense of the importance of the Pacific in world affairs, and as realistic an understanding of the situation created by Japan's rise to power.

CHAPTER VI

DOLLAR DIPLOMACY

WHILE THE ADMINISTRATION WHICH FOLLOWED that of President Roosevelt did not introduce any new elements into our Far Eastern policy, its attitude was based upon a more frank avowal of the importance of trade interests than any preceding Administration had ever made. President Taft and his Secretary of State, Philander C. Knox, were forthright advocates of dollar diplomacy. They made themselves the aggressive champions of those commercial and financial interests in this country which interpreted the Open Door as an invitation to seize for themselves whatever opportunities China offered for the investment of American capital or the expansion of American commerce.

Both Hay and Roosevelt had endeavored to further American trade, but they had more directly sought to promote American political power and prestige in the Far East. Roosevelt had used the opportunity offered by the Russo-Japanese War to assert American influence in international affairs throughout the world. His intervention in that conflict had been closely followed by his participation in the Algeciras Conference and attempt to exercise a balance of power in purely European politics.

President Taft's outlook was more limited in its scope from the international point of view, and far more concerned with immediately practical objectives. "While foreign policy should not be turned a hair's breadth from the straight path of justice," he stated on one occasion, "it may well be made to include active intervention to secure for our merchandise and our capitalists opportunities for profitable investment." And by active intervention he meant exactly what he said. This he had made clear in his inaugural address. America could secure respect for her just demands in the Orient, he declared, but she could not do so "if it is understood that she never intends to back up her assertion of right and her defense of interest by anything but mere verbal protest and diplomatic notes."

Secretary Knox was even more frankly of the dollar-diplomacy school as demonstrated by his policy both in the Far East and in Latin America. His conception of his rôle in the Government was that it offered him a chance to represent his clients, business and finance, in a wider sphere than when he had served them as a corporation lawyer in private practice.

These theories prepared the ground for a policy of economic penetration in China which went far beyond anything which had heretofore been projected. They provided the encouragement for a more serious effort to establish dominant economic influence in the Orient than Hay or Roosevelt had ever envisaged. The underlying idea behind the Open Door policy had been that with a free field and no favor America could outmaneuver her commercial rivals in the Far East. The attempt was now to be made to apply this theory.

The degree to which this policy conflicted with Japan's aims and aspirations was never fully understood by the Taft Administration. But the Tokyo Government realized it immediately. Indeed, Japan met American efforts to offset her dominant position in Manchuria in such determined fashion that here the State Department was forced to beat a hurried retreat. For there was already this basic difference between the policy of Japan and that of America: Japan knew exactly what she wanted and was prepared to use force to support her position, while the United States was not quite sure of what it wanted and public opinion would not sanction the use of force.

Watching developments from the sidelines, Roosevelt characterized his successor's program in its relation to Japan as one "combining irritation and inefficiency." He had followed the development of Japanese policy; he had a healthy respect for Japanese ambition. The moderate course he had pursued at the time of the San Francisco school-board incident, and the conclusion of the Root-Takahira Agreement, both attested his realistic appraisal of Japan's attitude.

Nor did he hesitate to make his views known to Taft. In an oft-quoted letter written in December, 1910, he bluntly declared that if Japan chose to follow a course in Manchuria to which the United States was averse, she could only be stopped by war. And the United States was not prepared for such a war.

"The Open Door policy in China was an excellent thing," Roosevelt wrote, "and I hope it will be a good thing for the future, so far as it can be maintained by general diplomatic agreement; but . . . the Open Door policy, as a matter of fact, completely disappears as soon as a powerful nation determines to disregard it, and is willing to run the risk of war rather than forego its intention."

While subsequent events have proved how indisputably right Roosevelt was, the Taft Administration did not take his advice. In its zeal to promote American financial and commercial activities in the Far East, it completely disregarded Japanese interests. The growing conviction of Japan that the United States was the real obstacle to that expansion on the Asiatic mainland to which she was so firmly committed was thus immeasurably strengthened.

A first and important attempt to promote American interests in China involved the State Department in the complicated raiiway politics of Manchuria. It developed from a move first initiated during the Russo-Japanese War by one of the outstanding Wall Street figures of the period, E. H. Harriman, whose fertile imagination had conceived the grandiose scheme of controlling a round-the-world transportation system. In conjunction with his trans-Pacific steamship lines, he planned to secure control of the Manchurian railways connecting with the Trans-Siberia Railway, and then acquire trackage rights over this Russian road to provide the necessary link with Western Europe.

In order "to save the commercial interest of the United States from being entirely wiped from the Pacific Ocean," as he patriotically phrased it, the New York financier had approached the Japanese Government with his scheme while the war with Russia was still in progress. He offered to reconstruct the railways in South Manchuria in return for a half interest in their management.

Railways were the means to both political and commercial power in Manchuria, and no phase of international relations in the Far East was more complex than railway politics. Russia had early won permission to extend the Trans-Siberia Railway through Manchuria and constructed the Chinese Eastern Railway from Manchouli to Suijenko; she had subsequently wrested a concession to extend this line south from Harbin to Port Arthur. Her position in Manchuria was largely predicated on railway control. Through her military victories Japan had then fallen heir to the railways in South Manchuria, and their possession constituted Japan's principal means for asserting her new influence in the territories they served.

Under such circumstances the strangest thing about the Harriman incident was that his proposal was at all considered by the Japanese Government. Nevertheless it won the approval of Marquis Ito and of Premier Katsura. Their apparent willingness to share control of the South Manchuria railway system with American financial interests is, indeed, sometimes cited as evidence that Japan did not yet harbor aggressive designs against this Chinese territory.

But the Government's attitude changed quickly. Upon Foreign Minister Komura's return from the Portsmouth Conference late in 1905, entirely different counsels prevailed in the Japanese high command. On the pretense that Japan had to get China's approval to reorganize the South Manchuria Railway, but actually because the Japanese Government had no idea of shar-

ing management of this new company with the nationals of any other country, the Harriman-Katsura
memorandum was shelved.

The round-the-world transportation system nevertheless remained a dream which Harriman could not forget. Unable to get control of the South Manchuria Railway, he played with the idea of constructing a new line
generally paralleling it, and interested himself in the
possibility of securing from the Chinese a concession
for such an undertaking.

In this project he had both an enthusiastic and able
coadjutor in the American consul-general in Mukden,
Willard Straight. No stronger advocate of any program
which would extend American interests in the Orient
and tend to block further Japanese encroachments upon
China could have been found. When Taft had visited
Manchuria in the summer of 1907 in his rôle of Secretary of War, Straight eagerly attempted to impress upon
him the importance of encouraging American investment in the Far East. He was so sure he had succeeded
that he happily confided to his diary that he had persuaded Taft to advise the Administration "to regard
Manchuria as a fair field and not as one which must
be approached with special regard for the susceptibili-
ties of the Japanese."

Straight was a striking example of that useful union
of idealism and practicality which characterized American policy in Asia. He felt keenly that the United States
should take a strong stand to protect China's independence; he pictured his rôle as that of a knight-errant
prepared to do battle for democracy and uphold the
weak against the strong. But he also made himself, for

EDWARD H. HARRIMAN

WILLARD D. STRAIGHT

all his official position as consul-general, a direct agent of American capitalism. On this distant frontier of international finance, he was continually zealous to open up every possible avenue for investment which would serve to entrench America more firmly in the Far East.

To this end he worked out a plan with the Chinese officials for creation of a bank which would finance the railway construction contemplated by Harriman, together with other projects for the development of Manchuria by American capital, and he soon had a definite agreement ready for submission to the New York financier. The happy event was enthusiastically recorded in his diary on August 7, 1907: "Tang approved draft. Letter mailed! Fraught with tremendous possibilities. If adopted it means we play principal part in the development of Manchuria. Our influence in China tremendously enhanced."

The letter reached New York something more than a month later, but it could not have arrived at a less propitious time. Wall Street was in the nervous grip of approaching financial panic. The Stock Exchange was floundering. Even Harriman could hardly hope to win support and raise the funds for building a railway in China. Once again his ambitious scheme for a round-the-world transportation system was balked.

Straight was bitterly disappointed, but he continued to do everything he could to keep the field open for American investment and prevent Japan from closing the market. He took it upon himself, although holding consular office, to urge the Chinese to form a publicity bureau to attract foreign capital to Manchuria. Through his assistant, who resigned from the consular service to head the bureau, he actively coöperated in its propaganda.

Moreover he maintained his contacts with Governor Tang, and as circumstances became more favorable for the scheme disrupted by the American financial panic, he reached a new tentative agreement for a $20,000,000 loan to finance railroad construction and promote Manchurian mining, timber, and agricultural development. Harriman was still interested in this project, and on his suggestion an obliging State Department sent for Straight to report in person on the general situation in Manchuria as a field for investment.

Having twice failed, Straight and Harriman now had every reason to believe that the railway concession they sought was within their grasp. Governor Tang had arranged to follow Straight to Washington to negotiate a final contract, and the necessary funds were available. But a series of unfortunate coincidences intervened to block completion of the new program even more effectively than Japanese opposition and financial panic had blocked Harriman's previous plans.

Most important was the conclusion of the Root-Takahira Agreement. It was just at this time—November, 1908—that the notes embodying this statement of policy were being exchanged, and their recognition of the status quo in Manchuria made the occasion anything but favorable for official American sponsorship of a project which Japan would naturally resent as an infringement of her special rights. "A terrible diplomatic blunder to be laid at the door of T. R.," Straight sadly noted in his diary.

At the same time, the position of Governor Tang

had been greatly weakened through governmental changes in China which had followed the death, in mid-November, of both the Empress Dowager and the Emperor, and other negotiations on the part of both British and American financiers for the construction of a Chinese Government railroad between Chinchow and Aiguin had further served to complicate an already confused situation. An agreement had actually been signed for this Chinchow-Aiguin line, when the death of Harriman brought to a final end the more ambitious project for a complete round-the-world system.

The Taft Administration, coming into office in March, 1909, nevertheless considered these developments both interesting and important. It felt that a real issue was at stake in Manchuria, and it was fully determined, despite the Root-Takahira Agreement, to do what it could to support American capitalism. But in reviewing the conflicting aims and aspirations of the various Powers, with both American and British capitalists seeking concessions whch were strongly opposed by Japan, Secretary Knox had a new idea. It occurred to him that complete neutralization of the Manchurian railways held out a solution of the problem which would most effectively protect existing American interests and allow a free field for the further investment of American capital.

To this end he officially suggested, in November, a comprehensive scheme which would bring "the Manchurian highways and the railroads under an economic and scientific and impartial administration by some plan vesting in China the ownership of the railroads through funds furnished for that purpose by the interested Powers willing to participate. . . . The plan should provide that the nationals of the participating Powers should supervise the railroad systems during the terms of the loan."

In many respects the Knox program for the commercial neutralization of Manchuria was the most practical possible application of the Open Door policy. But it completely ignored the realities of the situation. For it should have been clear that it was not likely Russia would approve, and that under no circumstances could Japan accede to a proposal which would have so completely blocked the attainment of all her ambitions.

Nevertheless Knox made no attempt to discover how such a proposal would be received by the most interested governments. Paying no attention to a polite hint from Great Britain that, in view of other loan negotiations, it would be wiser to postpone consideration of his project, he went blithely ahead. The American envoys in Japan and Russia were instructed to present the plan formally to the governments to which they were accredited, and an optimistic statement was given out by the State Department.

In the American press the scheme was characterized as "startling for its audacity" and was said "to strike the pick into the very heart of the Far Eastern Question." Europe termed it impractical and utopian, hinting also that the United States had now become a suitor for the territory over which Russia and Japan had so lately fought. From Tokyo came more critical comment.

"It is nothing but selfish ambition and unreasonable jealousy," one Japanese paper said, "which actuated her [America] to propose in the name of international peace, the neutralization of Manchurian railways." Count Hayashi was quoted as saying that it amounted to "confiscation by the Powers of Japan's rights in Manchuria, secured as a reward of the heavy expenditure of blood and treasure."

The issue, of course, was one which primarily concerned Russia and Japan—Russia as owner of the Chinese Eastern Railway, and Japan as owner of the South Manchuria Railway. For a time neither Power replied to Secretary Knox's proposals. When at last they did, it was clear that they had agreed upon a common policy. The neutralization program was summarily rejected. Russia flatly stated that it would "seriously injure Russian interests both public and private, to which the Imperial Government attached great importance." Japan declared she could not see "in the present condition of things in Manchuria anything so exceptional as to make it necessary or desirable to set up there an exceptional system not required in other parts of China."

The principal effect of Secretary Knox's ill-advised attempt to intervene in Manchuria was thus to throw together Russia and Japan, so lately enemies, in mutual defense of their respective spheres of influence in Northern and Southern Manchuria. There was no chance, there had been no chance, of according Manchuria a quasi-neutral status.

Even the original railway concession obtained by American capitalists had to be abandoned in the face of this opposition. For in view of secret protocols wherein China had agreed not to construct any railway parallel to the Japanese-owned lines, Tokyo asserted, and was prepared to enforce, the right to control all railway construction in South Manchuria. The United States could protest, and it did so, but that was all.

If this was a signal defeat for American policy in the Orient, Secretary Knox was able to point to what appeared to be a more successful application of dollar diplomacy in certain loan negotiations which were being concurrently conducted with the Chinese Government in Peking. To fully as great an extent as in Manchuria, the Taft Administration here demonstrated its full support for capitalist enterprise in China.

Willard Straight was again the agent for the American financiers in these negotiations. He had shown such zeal in seeking out concessions in Manchuria that they had eagerly commissioned him to represent their interests in the frantic hunt for new fields of investment. While he had resigned from the consular service, the close relationship between American finance and the State Department gave him almost an official standing in his new rôle in Peking.

His first task involved possible American participation in the so-called Hukuang loan for the construction of a railroad which would tap the rich resources of the western province of Szechuan.

This loan had been initiated by Great Britain, France, and Germany. The United States was being left out. Obviously the lending Powers would be in a position to exercise a powerful influence in the economic development of the provinces served by the projected railroad, and American interests might well be at their mercy. In these circumstances President Taft was prevailed upon to take the unprecedented step of appealing directly to the Prince Regent of China for the admission of American capital in the proposed loan.

"I have an intense personal interest," the President cabled some four months after his inauguration in 1909, "in making the use of American capital in the development of China an instrument for the promotion of the welfare of China, and an increase in her material prosperity without entanglements or creating embarrassments affecting the growth of her independent political power and the preservation of her territorial integrity."

Under such pressure both China and the interested Powers were compelled to accept American participation. Straight was empowered to go ahead with the difficult and protracted negotiations which agreement with the Chinese Government and the representatives of the various banking groups necessitated.

A four-Power consortium—the United States, Great Britain, France, and Germany—was organized to handle this loan, and also to take up the further and even more important project of a currency loan which would enable the Chinese Government to establish some order in the chaotic financial condition in which it found itself. Here again Straight was accorded the complete backing of the American State Department. There were times when he did not feel that Washington fully realized how important were the stakes for American capital. "Do they think we are playing kindergarten games," he impatiently wrote on one occasion, "instead of gambling for an empire?" But he actually had little cause for complaint in the attitude of either President Taft or Secretary Knox.

An agreement was finally reached. The Chinese Government accepted the terms jointly agreed upon by the international bankers. Straight was triumphant. "Dollar diplomacy is justified at last," he wrote home exultantly. He saw China's position greatly strengthened, American influence firmly established. With his usual enthusiasm he characterized the agreement as the "first tangible result of the new policy inaugurated by Secretary Knox."

But events had little respect for the triumphs of dollar diplomacy. No sooner had the final arrangements for the currency loan been completed in April, 1911, than China was swept by revolution. The Manchu Dynasty collapsed. To the astonishment of the world, a precarious republic rose from the ashes of the dying Empire.

The international bankers for a time did not know where to turn. They saw all their plans and hopes disappointed. Straight had himself been slow in recognizing the importance of the revolutionary movement. He had been prepared to make an immediate loan to the tottering Manchu régime in the belief that it could then suppress the disorders throughout the Empire. Things had moved too fast, however, for any such action. The foreign capitalists had then somewhat belatedly recognized that their real opportunity for investing capital in China was in a reorganization loan to the new republican government.

To this end the consortium was reconstructed, this time with the inclusion of Japan and Russia, who were clamoring for participation in a loan which had such important possibilities. Negotiations were started with the new régime under strict conditions whereby the foreign banking groups were to have virtually full control over Chinese finances to insure the security of their investment. The new government had nowhere else to turn and was prepared, in the early months of 1913, to make the necessary concessions for a loan of from forty to sixty million pounds.

At this point President Wilson came into office. Representatives of the American banking group, as a matter of form, sought from the new Administration the official blessing on their activities which had been so gladly extended by President Taft. To their startled surprise, it was not forthcoming.

In complete repudiation of his predecessor's policy, Wilson announced, only some two weeks after his inauguration, that he felt the terms of the proposed loan infringed upon China's sovereignty. The United States would not assume the responsibility for this indirect intervention in her internal affairs. "Our interests are those of the Open Door," the President stated emphatically, "a door of friendship and mutual advantage. This is the only door we care to enter."

With such complete abandonment of official support, the American bankers felt compelled to withdraw. Some years later President Wilson was to revive the consortium—in somewhat different guise—but at this time the terms of its proposed loan to China violated his conception of what our support for China's independence should really mean. He would have none of his predecessor's dollar diplomacy.

Viewed in retrospect, the Knox railroad neutralization scheme for Manchuria and the forcible injection of American capital into the proposed international loans to the Chinese Government constitute a strange chapter in the history of American relations in the Far East. Never has so-called national interest been more closely identified with economic imperialism. The State Department not only offered unlimited support to the representatives of American capitalism; it made them the spear-head of American policy in the Orient.

In his biography of Willard Straight, Herbert Croly wrote that the promoters of the consortium foresaw the day when the relation of the United States to the economic development and political welfare of China would become the major preoccupation of American foreign policy. "The attempt to anticipate that day," he further said, "and commit the United States to an immediately active participation in Chinese affairs was born of a thoroughly sound analysis of the part which we would have to play in the future regional policies of the Pacific."

Certainly there has been no time when our policy has been more definitely predicated upon the theory that in the course of national expansion, America must of necessity look to the Orient for a profitable field for investment and trade. The Taft Administration was convinced that the United States was in a measure dependent upon the Far East, and that we consequently could not afford to allow Japan to dominate this vast and relatively unexploited area of the world's surface.

That the other Powers, and not Japan alone, believed our activity actuated by something more than the pure altruism toward China in which we liked to clothe it, was generally recognized by observers in the Far East.

Early in 1912, Secretary Knox received a dispatch from our minister in Peking which recorded the prevailing impression in the Chinese capital that the United States had been pursuing an "active and aggressive policy, which is competitive if not hostile to all other foreign interests in China."

This comment, however, was not made in criticism of dollar diplomacy. It was made to stress the point that if this policy was to be successful, it would have to be even more strongly upheld than it had been. At best it would be extremely difficult to enforce the American interpretation of the Open Door, wrote the American minister, but without full public backing, it would be hopeless. "Diplomacy," he stated, "however astute, however beneficial and altruistic it may be, if it is not supported by the force which not only commands but demands respect and consideration, will avail but little."

But even in the period 1909-13, the golden era of dollar diplomacy, there was no such pronounced national interest in the Far East. Certainly there was no support for any policy of force. Dollar diplomacy largely failed of its objectives because the American people could not be prevailed upon to give it the sanction sought by the Taft Administration.

CHAPTER VII

WHILE EUROPE WAS AT WAR

WHILE THE INTERNATIONAL RELATIONS OF THE FAR
East remained immensely complicated by these
railroad and banking problems in the first year of the
Wilson Administration, events of far greater importance
were shaping to a crisis on the other side of the world.
For in mid-summer of 1914 a shot was fired at Sarajevo.
Alarms and excursions swept over Europe; the armies
of the West marched to war. But it was in a sense *Der
Tag* for Japan as well as for Germany. It was that opportunity, long foreseen by such statesmen as Viscount
Tani and Count Hayashi. It was "the time of the confusion of Europe" when Japan might hope to put the
meddling Powers in their place. The Tokyo Government immediately took the aggressive, and embarked
on a determined attempt to attain a position on the
Asiatic mainland which would compel recognition of
Japan's paramount power in the Orient.

A first opportunity was presented by the fortunate
coincidence that Japan was an ally of Great Britain,
through the Anglo-Japanese Alliance, and that England's enemy had in the province of Shantung a territorial base which Japan could easily attack. Her obligations under the Anglo-Japanese Alliance did not demand any such action. While England welcomed Jap-

anese aid against possible German naval operations in
the Pacific, she actually endeavored to persuade Japan
not to declare war against Germany and not to undertake military measures against Shantung. The stability
of the Far East appeared to Great Britain a more important objective, and she was exceedingly apprehensive
of possible repercussions of Japanese participation in
the war.

Japan could not be dissuaded. An attack on Germany's possessions in China afforded her a chance to
revenge herself on that country for its interference in
Japan's plans in 1894. The occupation of Tsingtao, German leasehold in Shantung, could be used as a lever to
exert more influence over China. While Europe's armies
entered upon their death struggle in Northern France,
Japanese ships and men moved upon Shantung. In
November, 1914, Tsingtao fell before their concerted
attack.

If Great Britain was fearful that Japanese participation in the World War would encourage an aggressive
policy toward China, the Chinese Government was
convinced of it. President Yuan Shih-Kai believed that
Japan sought not only Shantung but Manchuria. On
October 2, 1914, he told the American minister in
Peking that Tokyo had "a definite and far-reaching plan
for using the European crisis to further an attempt to
lay the foundation of control over China." And even
though he then had no public proof that this was indeed
Japan's policy, the somewhat ambiguous statements
made by Foreign Minister Kato in regard to the status
of Tsingtao served to substantiate his theory.

For while Count Kato declared that Japan had no

designs upon the territory of any third Power, and that she remained firmly wedded to the principle of the Open Door, he would make no definite commitment as to the restoration of German territory to China. It was a question to be settled in the future, he told the Japanese Diet, and at the same time he strongly intimated that the Government was contemplating decisive measures to settle the entire question of Japan's relations with China.

The United States regarded these developments in the Far East with some misgiving. Japanese assurances that American interests in China would in no way be affected did not entirely lull the suspicions of those observers whose attention could be diverted from the more dramatic events taking place in Europe. "There is a general belief," editorialized the New York *Times*, "that it is the policy of Japan to assert and maintain for herself supremacy and control in the Asiatic waters of the Pacific with a view, probably, to the ultimate exclusion of the influence of Western nations."

Nevertheless there was in Washington a firm determination not to become embroiled in the Far East. The attitude of the Wilson Administration was clearly expressed in a statement by Acting Secretary of State Lansing that "it would be quixotic in the extreme to allow the question of China's territorial integrity to entangle the United States in international difficulties."

The issue arose, indeed, at a time when the background of American-Japanese relations made the danger of such entanglement very real. While the United States was affronted by the evidence which Japanese activities

on the Asiatic mainland offered of an aggressive imperialism which might threaten American interests in
the entire Pacific area, Japan had harbored a growing
resentment against American policy in the Far East ever
since the Knox program for neutralization of the Manchuria railroads. In the period 1913-15 there were recurrent flare-ups on both sides of the Pacific of the jingoistic spirit which had first been in evidence in 1906-08.
There was a revival of the war talk of those earlier days.

A first sign of this war hysteria was evident early in
1913. Japan became aroused over a recrudescence of
the anti-Japanese feeling in California induced by the
immigration problem, or rather by the status of Japanese immigrants on the West Coast, which had led
to the passage of a law specifically prohibiting the Japanese from owning any land in the state. So violent was
the popular reaction in Japan to this California legislation that in Washington a worried Cabinet gravely
contemplated the possibility of the issue leading to hostilities. Secretary of War Garrison suggested immediate
measures for the defense of the Philippines.

But there was in the Wilson Cabinet one man whose
strong pacifism was never affected by mob hysteria or
the outcries of special interests. William Jennings Bryan
immediately flared up at this proposal.

"He got red in the face and was very emphatic,"
wrote another member of the Cabinet, David F. Hous-
ton. "He thundered out that army and navy officers
could not be trusted to say what we should or should
not do, till we actually got into war; that we were
not discussing how to wage war, but how not to get into

war, and that, if ships were moved in the East, it would incite to war."

President Wilson agreed with his Secretary of State. There was no movement of ships. Japan's protest against the land laws was answered by a conciliatory note, and every effort made to assuage her wounded feelings. But while official moderation in both Washington and Tokyo thus averted what might have developed into a serious crisis, American public opinion had been aroused over the angry recriminations voiced in Japan. Fed by alarmist stories that as a consequence of our stand upon immigration, the Japanese Government was planning drastic action, the West professed to believe that Japan was actually seeking a foothold on the American continent.

If the Hearst papers of the period could be believed, Japan was about to seize California. Negotiations on the part of a Japanese syndicate to purchase a tract of land in Magdalena Bay, in Lower California, were magnified into an attempt to acquire a naval base. The beaching of a ship in Turtle Bay, also in Lower California, was the basis for an exposure of a sensational Japanese plot to attack the West Coast. Even the New York *Herald* took up the exciting story with lurid details of war-ships concentrating, harbors mined, and the landing of troops.

Timid Californians trembled in their boots, conjured up fantastic visions of impending invasion, and fearfully sang:

> They've battle-ships, they say,
> On Magdalena Bay!
> Uncle Sam, won't you listen when we warn you?

Needless to say, there was no real basis for these absurd reports. They were propaganda engineered by special interests for their own purposes: politicians fomenting the anti-Japanese agitation to win votes, armament manufacturers drumming up big navy sentiment, and newspapers out to gain circulation. The rumors were so insistent, however, that the chairman of the House Committee on Foreign Relations stated his conviction that there was a criminal conspiracy on foot to bring about war.

Widespread publicity was also given to various statements by Japanese leaders which appeared to strengthen the theory that Japan was preparing to attack America. Prince Ito was quoted as having forecast a great European war to be followed by a struggle for the mastery of the Pacific. A statement was culled from the Japan *Year Book* declaring that the expansion in Japanese armaments was "primarily to guard our interests in Manchuria and China, and next to be prepared against a possible emergency with the United States." As noted an authority on the Far East as Thomas Millard wrote in the *Century Magazine* that Japan was making deliberate preparation "in anticipation, if not actually in expectation, of a collision with the United States."

The very titles of books and magazine articles dealing with Japan indicated the nervous temper of public opinion. *Japan's Place in the Sun, The Menace of Japan, At the Edge of the Pit, The Japanese Crisis* were among the books which helped to spread war scares, while typical of magazine articles were "Racial War in the Pacific," "Inevitable War Between the United States and Japan," "The Japanese War Scare," "Playing with

Dynamite," and "The World's Most Menacing Problem."

Friends of peace attempted to counteract the flood of provocative literature. In 1914 the Japan Society issued *Japan's Message to America,* in which thirty Japanese leaders poured oil on the seething waters, and a year later the pacifistic statements of fifty-two American spokesmen were incorporated in *America to Japan.* But while sober students of history might realize that whatever Japan's ambitions in the Far East, the idea of her attacking America was fantastic, reason could not entirely dissipate the popular effect of such Hearst paper head-lines as

THE ONE VAST MENACE TO THE UNITED STATES:
Japan Steadily Pursues Preparations for War.

America was thus in no friendly mood toward Japan in 1914 and regarded with deep suspicion every step she made. Nor did we have long to wait after the capture of Tsingtao for further evidence of her aggressive tactics. She naturally enough never entertained any idea of launching an attack upon California, but expansion in Asia was a different matter altogether. There she steadily pursued her imperialistic policy. Continuing to take advantage of the world's preoccupation with the European conflict, she went grimly ahead with a program for which preparations had long been made.

The armies of Europe were deadlocked in the frozen trenches of Northern France; Italy was still wavering between throwing in her lot with the Allies or with the Central Powers, when in January, 1915, Tokyo suddenly and secretly presented the Chinese Government with a series of demands for which history offers no parallel in brutal audacity. Known ever since as the Twenty-One Demands, they were divided into five general groups:

The first attempted to secure for Japan a free hand in Shantung.

The second provided for the extension of the rights and privileges then held in Manchuria over a ninety-nine year period, together with certain extensions of those rights.

The third stipulated the granting of certain mining concessions.

The fourth involved the recognition of Japan's special position in the province of Fukien.

The fifth contemplated, among other special privileges, the appointment of Japanese advisers to the Chinese Government, China's purchase of 50 per cent or more of her munitions of war from Japan, and joint Sino-Japanese administration of the police departments of important cities.

Obviously, acceptance of these terms would have resulted in China's complete subservience to Japanese control and the establishment of a virtual protectorate. Even Japanese historians have not hesitated to characterize the Twenty-One Demands as a direct violation of China's sovereignty. But at the time, Tokyo made every effort to justify its action as a necessary move to settle various outstanding problems and to place relations with China on a stable basis.

So unjustified and unprovoked did the demands appear to the world at large that even the European Governments turned aside from their own critical problems

to hold up their hands in holy horror at this undisguised
assault upon China. But they could not worry about
the Far East for very long. Their own right to life was
of more immediate moment than that of China. Japan
had indeed chosen a time to act when the Powers could
do little more than protest in pained surprise at the
aptitude with which she had learned the imperialistic
lessons they themselves had taught her.

In the United States there was the popular outburst
which might have been expected from such a direct
affront to both our material and idealistic interests in
China. Japan had exposed her villainy. We had seen it
coming: the restrictions on trade in Manchuria, the rejection of the Knox neutralization scheme, the seizure
of Shantung. But the Twenty-One Demands were
deemed to constitute a challenge to our policy in the
Far East beside which these previous threats were in-
significant. They were a contemptuous denial of the
whole concept of the Open Door.

Nevertheless public opinion was confused. There was
no clear-cut indication of what we should do. While
the New York *Sun* emphatically stated that "this country cannot by any possibility let Japan's forward movement go by default," other representative papers were
quoted by the *Literary Digest* as saying that they were
"not inclined to urge their government on to any conflict with Japan." Secretary Bryan, as pacifistic in 1915
as he had been in 1913, took no other step than the dispatch of a moderate note to Tokyo quietly pointing out
the implications of the demands and their effect upon
the Open Door.

The marked evidence of world disapproval served in

some measure to abate Japan's zeal. It has been recorded by a Japanese historian that the Genro, or Elder Statesmen, insisted "that particular caution and moderation should be exercised not to arouse the suspicion abroad that advantage was being taken of the helpless situation in China and of the World War," and on these grounds the parliamentary opposition took occasion to attack the Cabinet for pursuing too openly an aggressive policy.

In a resolution which received the support of 130 members, the negotiations with China were declared inappropriate in every respect, detrimental to the amicable relationship between the two countries, and provocative of suspicions on the part of the Powers. "They have the effect of lowering the prestige of the Japanese Empire," it was said. ". . . Far from capable of establishing the foundations of peace in the Far East, they will form the source of future trouble."

As a result of this pressure, both at home and abroad, application of the fifth group of demands was withheld. But neither the moderating influence of the Genro, nor opposition within the Diet, wholly political in origin, served to deflect the Government from its main objective. And in so far as this program contemplated the firm and unquestioned establishment of Japanese influence in Manchuria and Shantung, there was no question that the country as a whole supported it. Foreign Minister Kato was pursuing one step further the basic, underlying motive of Japanese foreign policy since the Russo-Japanese War. Consequently when the Chinese endeavored to find some means to avoid compliance with these harsh terms, an ultimatum was dispatched to Peking, and preparations were made for a general mobilization. China thereupon capitulated and accepted under duress the modified demands.

Seventeen years later, when Japan again took advantage of a period which found the Western World intensely absorbed in its own affairs to make an even more aggressive attack upon Chinese sovereignty, the United States refused to recognize any treaty or agreement which impaired American rights or had been concluded contrary to existing treaty obligations. The Stimson Doctrine was hailed as a new departure in international law, establishing a new precedent in international relations. But except for the inclusion in existing treaty obligations of the provisions of the Kellogg anti-war treaty, Secretary Stimson's notes to China and Japan in 1932 bore a striking similarity to those which Secretary Bryan sent to China and Japan in 1915.

For it was in the earlier year that the United States first stated that it could not "recognize any agreement or undertaking which has been entered into or which may be entered into between the governments of Japan and China, impairing the treaty rights of the United States and its citizens in China, the political or territorial integrity of the Republic of China, or the international policy relative to China, commonly known as the Open Door policy."

In making this declaration of policy upon conclusion of the Sino-Japanese negotiations, Secretary Bryan was merely putting the position of the United States on record. It had no more direct bearing than this on the course of events in the Far East. It indicated that in a certain sense we considered China our ward, and there-

fore refused to give our blessing to any forced marriage
with Japan, but there was no indication that we were
going to do anything further about it. Just as was later
to happen in regard to Manchukuo, this policy disappointed China because she expected more of us, and
enraged Japan because she considered the affair none
of our business.

With China compelled to accept Japan's paramount influence in Manchuria and Shantung, the
Tokyo Government thereupon proceeded to consolidate
the gains won through the Twenty-One Demands. It
undertook to strengthen its position against the possible,
if unlikely, contingency of America making her opposition felt more strongly than through polite protests.
She turned first to Russia, as she had when the United
States attempted to undermine her position in Manchuria through railway neutralization, and in 1916 a
treaty was concluded with that Power for the mutual
defense of their interests and special rights in the Far
East.

Moreover this accord, as was subsequently disclosed,
was supplemented by a secret military alliance. The Japanese and Russian Governments agreed that their vital
interests required the safeguarding of China from the
possible political dominion of any third Power which
might have hostile designs against either Russia or
Japan. The alliance stipulated that in the event of a
declaration of war against either signatory by such a
third Power, because of measures which Japan or Russia might take to defend their special interests in China,
they would come to each other's aid.

The identity of the nation against which this treaty of alliance was directed admits of no question. Germany had been driven from the Orient. It could hardly have been one of the two Powers' European allies. Japan was very definitely bulwarking her position against America. Not much more than a decade earlier, the United States had tacitly supported Japan in her war to drive Russia from South Manchuria. Now these two former enemies, driven into each other's arms by our own policy, were allied to protect themselves against our possible interference in their respective spheres of influence.

The United States had no knowledge of this secret military alliance. While it was clearly evident that Russia and Japan had a very real community of interests, there was no reason to suspect an agreement for obligatory military assistance.

Japan also concluded, shortly after this, a series of secret treaties with her European allies whereby they agreed to recognize her rights in Shantung at the close of the war, and also her title to the German islands in the Pacific north of the equator. Here again the United States was in ignorance of how definitely Japan was insuring her wartime gains in Eastern Asia. But this acknowledgment on the part of the Allies that Japan was the rightful heir to all German interests in China was to have wide repercussions when the war settlements came to be made at Versailles.

With her arrangements so neatly made and the rewards of her continued allegiance to the Allied cause so fully guaranteed, Japan's program was quietly to await the final Allied victory over Germany. Consequently the events of 1917 were not altogether to her liking. For when they brought both the United States and China into the war, thereby entitling them to seats at the prospective peace conference, Japan foresaw an opposition to her carefully laid plans which might not otherwise have materialized.

This attitude was exemplified in the feeling expressed in Japan when America urged China to follow her example and declare war on Germany. On at least two occasions the Tokyo Government had definitely vetoed proposals that China adopt the Allied cause, and the pressure exercised by President Wilson to bring about a change in this policy was consequently judged a direct affront to Japan.

Public opinion in that country took the ground that the United States had no right to intervene so directly in China's affairs. It assailed President Wilson for assuming to offer the Chinese Government advice. And an irritated press declared that the United States should not take such a step without first consulting the Japanese Foreign Office. So far had Japan advanced in the belief that she was entitled to consider China a protectorate.

Naturally enough this evidence of continuing rivalry and antagonism in the Far East did not make for that friendly feeling between the two non-European adherents of the Allied cause most conducive to full international coöperation. The two nominal allies were on precarious ground. Once again reading the sensational press, the American public might have been excused for some confusion as to whether Japan was friend or foe.

The Governments of both countries recognized the risks inherent in this situation, and Japan soon made an important move, with the double objective of placating public opinion in this country, and of attempting to win American recognition of her new position in the Orient. Only the first objective was openly admitted, but the latter was suspected by more realistic observers. "We are the subjects of a diplomatic drive," Jeremiah W. Jenks wrote in the *Economic World*, "of which the objective is our recognition of Japan as the paramount power guaranteeing a Monroe Doctrine to Asia."

The instrument to achieve this purpose was a special mission to the United States headed by Viscount Ishii. In the enthusiasm engendered by wartime propaganda, he was given a royal welcome. The doubts and misgivings as to Japan's policy were quickly forgotten. When Viscount Ishii eloquently declared that Japan voluntarily engaged not to violate China's independence and to observe fully the Open Door, there were few to question just what she was actually doing in Manchuria and Shantung.

America and Japan were allies. They were engaged in overthrowing imperialism, in making the world safe for democracy. It was easy to overlook the incongruity of Japan battling at America's side in support of principles of political and international conduct which her own activities in the Far East expressly violated.

Viscount Ishii, in any event, sensed the mood of exaltation in which America found herself and judged the time particularly opportune for an adjustment of all outstanding questions. He took up with President

Wilson, and then with Secretary Lansing, the possibility of a mutual statement upon their policy toward China.

The negotiations which resulted in the Lansing-Ishii Agreement are shrouded in some mystery. Just as the two statesmen's interpretations of the significance of their final accord have disagreed, so have their accounts of their conversations. Viscount Ishii's objective was clear: recognition of Japan's "paramount interest" in China. According to his statements, Wilson was friendly to this thesis, but Lansing proved more difficult. The Secretary of State recognized the need for a joint declaration of policy, but he also felt it important to limit the agreement as strictly as possible to a reaffirmation of the Open Door.

It is possible that Japan brought strong pressure to bear upon American policy at this juncture by playing upon popular fears that she might not prove entirely faithful to the Allied cause. While there is no direct evidence of this, Ishii at least negatively drew attention to such a possibility. For he stated that on three occasions Germany had approached Japan with the idea that she might change her allegiance, but his Government had "firmly rejected the suggestion." Certainly the Japanese envoy convinced President Wilson that America should make a conciliatory gesture toward Japan for the sake of maintaining a strong, united front in the war emergency.

The result was a compromise. Lansing refused to accept the idea of "paramount influence" in China, but he did consent to embody in the agreement recognition of Japan's "special interests in China, particularly in the part to which her possessions are contiguous." It was a fine legal distinction. Its effect was to allow each party to the agreement to publicize his own interpretation of it.

In giving out the text in this country, Lansing studiously avoided any reference to "special interests" and emphasized that part of the agreement in which the United States and Japan mutually denied any aggressive designs in China and reaffirmed their faith in the Open Door. In subsequent testimony before the Senate Foreign Relations Committee, he stoutly declared that the controversial phrase meant nothing more than Japan's natural economic interests, derived solely from geographic propinquity.

On the other hand, Viscount Ishii maintained, both at the time and thereafter, that "special interests" had a far broader meaning and that the United States had in effect acknowledged that Japan had a special position in Manchuria because of her geographical, economic, and political relations. Moreover, this was the interpretation of the agreement insisted upon in the Far East. It was presented to China as definite evidence that America would no longer contest the extension of Japanese influence on the Asiatic mainland.

The Lansing-Ishii Agreement is today a closed incident; the misunderstandings it created led to its formal cancellation shortly after the Washington Conference six years later. But this does not detract from either its interest or importance. For if the Lansing-Ishii Agreement had been what the Japanese attempted to make it, and what its terminology at least suggested, it would have constituted a reversal of our traditional policy in

VISCOUNT ISHII AND SECRETARY OF STATE
ROBERT LANSING

the Far East. It would have implied abandonment of
the Open Door.

This was not the idea of the Wilson Administration,
so absorbed in European problems that the possible
implications of its essay in Far Eastern diplomacy were
hardly realized, but at the same time it was a logical
development of a policy which declared it to be
"quixotic in the extreme to allow the questions of
China's territorial integrity to entangle the United
States in international difficulties."

If recognition of Japan's special interests in China
had really replaced the doctrine of the Open Door, the
course of history in the Far East would have been
greatly changed. The basic conflict between America
and Japan might have been resolved and subsequent
controversies largely avoided. But this was hardly possible, even if such a change had been the Administration's goal, as the post-war reaction against the implications of the Lansing-Ishii Agreement and its eventual
cancellation clearly proved. America was not yet ready
to recognize Japan as the guardian of the peace of
the Far East, or to acknowledge her right to an Asiatic
Monroe Doctrine. The Open Door still had too strong
a hold upon popular imagination.

CHAPTER VIII

VERSAILLES

WHEN THE TIME AT LAST CAME FOR A WEARIED world to grapple with the immense problem of a peace treaty, America and Japan were both represented at Versailles. Far Eastern problems did not bulk very large beside the more momentous issue presented by the fate of Germany. They hardly existed as far as Europe was concerned. Nevertheless, Japan had no intention of allowing them to be forgotten, and came to Versailles to achieve a very definite objective: formal recognition of the new position she had succeeded in winning in Eastern Asia during the four years of European confusion.

America was prepared to contest strongly so sweeping a victory for Japan's interests in the Far East. Public opinion in this country still viewed with resentful suspicion the possible effect of her policy on our own position in the Pacific area. The Open Door was a definite part of the national credo. But at Versailles the practical realism of Japan's stand was to win a striking victory over the vague idealism of President Wilson. The extent to which she achieved her aims carried her further in her program of imperialistic expansion than she had gone at any time since her defeat of Russia fifteen years earlier.

In contrast to Japan's immediate objectives, America

sought at the conference a world-wide peace, incorporating the ideals for which we had gone to war. We had entered the European conflict in part to protect the vast commerce which we had allowed to develop with the Allies, and in part because of a growing conviction that the Allies were fighting our battles as well as their own against the menace of German imperialism. A peace which would ensure maintenance of the post-war status quo appeared to promise continuance of the economic supremacy we had won while Europe was fighting, and also a world which we fondly believed would be safe for democracy. In the person of Woodrow Wilson the idealistic elements in our foreign policy were at this time very much in the ascendancy. The practical aspects of the application of our policy, whether in Asia or elsewhere, were entirely secondary.

To establish a League of Nations which might serve as a harbinger of a new international order was consequently President Wilson's primary goal. Its attainment was worth any sacrifice. When Japan made acceptance of her wartime expansion the price of her coöperation in forming the League, Wilson felt reluctantly compelled to recognize these gains. It was an ironic consequence of this situation that the concessions made to Japan, involving as they did a denial of the principles upon which the League was founded, contributed in no small measure to the rejection of the League by the American people.

This aspect of the rôle played by Far Eastern affairs in the formation of the League of Nations should not be overstressed. Nevertheless, public opinion never condoned President Wilson's acceptance of the cession of

Germany's rights in Shantung to Japan. Whatever his motives, Senator Lodge made a telling appeal to American idealism in his bitter condemnation of what he termed the President's abject surrender to Japanese militarism. Even though Japan promised eventually to return Shantung to China, the President's attitude on this issue greatly strengthened the hands of the League's opponents. They were able to turn his own weapons against him.

Apart from these indirect consequences, the renewed clash between the United States and Japan in the controversy over Shantung hardly served to strengthen the friendly feeling between the two countries which had grown out of their common participation in the World War. For while America now felt that Japan was resuming her program of imperialistic expansion, Japan naturally felt that America was obstructing the attainment of her legitimate aspirations. The conflict of interests in the Orient was again emphasized with an inevitable embitterment of popular feeling in both countries.

Before she presented her demand for the retention of all German territory seized during the war, both the leasehold in Shantung and the Pacific islands which lay north of the equator, Japan attempted to have incorporated in the Covenant of the new League of Nations the principle of racial equality. Recognition of her right to a status of absolute equality in every respect had been a goal ever since the West had fastened upon her the stigma of inferiority through its insistence upon exterritoriality. While the revision of the early treaties had removed this blot upon her honor, the restrictions imposed upon Japanese nationals in regard to immigration continued to offend national pride. Japan urged adoption of a clause in the League Covenant whereby all member nations would agree to accord the nationals of whatever country equal and just treatment, "making no distinctions, either in law or fact, on account of their race or nationality."

Baron Makino and Viscount Chinda, the two principal Japanese delegates at the conference, took up this question with both President Wilson and Colonel House. While the Americans recognized the validity of Japan's position, popular opposition to Japanese immigration in both the United States and the British Dominions made the issue an extremely thorny one. A compromise was sought through a formula which would satisfy Japan's pride, and yet not infringe upon the right of every League member to determine its own domestic policies. When Australia expressed very definite opposition to even this half-way measure, President Wilson undertook to dissuade the Japanese from insisting upon it. He took the ground that the equality of nations was a fundamental principle of the League, but that racial equality did not necessarily have any place in the Covenant and would be a needless cause of controversy.

Japan would not let the issue drop. Her delegates demanded full discussion and a vote in the League of Nations Commission. It consequently had to be taken, and the result was eleven to six in favor of Japan's contention. The question then arose as to whether unanimity was not necessary on such a point. As presiding officer of the Commission, President Wilson ruled that it was.

Japan perforce submitted to this decision, but the refusal to acknowledge racial equality was interpreted as an affront to her national dignity. President Wilson was furiously attacked in the Japanese press. "Hypocrite" and "transformed Kaiser" were among the more friendly characterizations, while one paper made the strange charge that he had "a female despot within him." Unquestionably, the decision on racial equality also stiffened Japan's resolve to insist at whatever cost upon obtaining her more concrete demands. Political conditions at home made this necessary even if the government had not itself been fully committed to such a policy. Japan considered herself the rightful heir to all German interests in the Far East, and retention of Shantung had become not only an end in itself but a symbol of foreign recognition of her supremacy in the Far East.

The Japanese delegates became "very stiff about it," in Wilson's somewhat mournful phrase, and in the very midst of the crisis created by Italy's threatened withdrawal from the conference, they presented what virtually amounted to an ultimatum. Unless the peace treaty specifically provided for Germany's unconditional cession to Japan of the leased territory of Kiauchow (Tsingtao), together with all other rights and privileges held by Germany in Shantung, Baron Makino and Viscount Chinda quietly let it be known that their orders from Tokyo were to follow Italy in quitting the conference.

Their legal claims to the territory were based upon

very specific grounds. Through the treaties signed in 1915, as a result of the Twenty-One Demands, and supplementary agreements concluded three years later, China had acknowledged Japan's title to all privileges held by Germany. Through the secret treaties signed in 1917, the Allies had likewise recognized it.

In refutation of these claims, China insisted that her declaration of war against Germany had abrogated all prior agreements in regard to territory over which China held sovereign rights, while the treaties concluded with Japan, consequent upon the Twenty-One Demands, were invalid because they had been signed under duress. The issue presented a nice problem in international law, but these were not the grounds upon which it was to be settled.

The opposition to granting Japan's demands came, of course, from the United States. President Wilson was not deeply interested in the Far East. He was not apparently concerned over the possible consequences of affording Japan so strong a foothold on Chinese territory. But he could not fail to see the incongruity between his conception of a peace founded on justice and the allocation to one ally of the territories of another, solely because in the stress of war Japan had obtained a promise that this would be her reward. In the moralistic field where he was so thoroughly at home, there could be no possible justification for this outright robbery of Chinese territory.

Moreover, Wilson was subjected to strong pressure to maintain a determined stand against Japan both by public opinion at home and by the other members of the American peace delegation. To admit Japan's contention and award her Shantung, wrote General Tasker H. Bliss, would be to abandon the democracy of China "to the domination of the Prussianized militarism of Japan." In that fine strain of idealism which made the American delegates such easy victims to the intrigues of the more realistic-minded delegates of other nations, General Bliss told the President that it couldn't be right to do wrong even in the interests of peace. "Peace is desirable," he wrote, "but there are things dearer than peace—justice and freedom."

Wilson went to the Japanese. He sent Colonel House to the Japanese. They were friendly and conciliatory. They listened quietly to the President's exposition of the theory that nations should think more of their duties toward each other than of their own rights. When the importance of maintaining the Open Door was brought up, they "assented and expressed benevolent intentions." But on the necessity for the unconditional cession of Shantung, they were adamant. If President Wilson could not recognize this, they would have to withdraw from the peace conference.

Two sessions of the Council of Four—reduced to a Council of Three by the absence of Premier Orlando— were held on April 22nd in a final effort to settle the issue. In the morning the Japanese stated their case; in the afternoon the Chinese took the floor. But it was a futile proceeding. Neither Lloyd George nor Clemenceau was interested. The question had long since been settled for them in the secret treaties their governments had concluded with Japan. There is no evidence that they had considered the possibility that China's entry into the war might have changed the situation.

At one point, when the Chinese had advanced the argument that their treaties with Japan in 1915 were invalid because they had been signed under duress, Lloyd George unexpectedly asked to what they were referring.

The minutes of the conference then state:

"President Wilson asked if Mr. Lloyd George had never heard of the twenty-one points.

"Mr. Lloyd George said he had not."

Ignorance of what Japan was actually trying to do in the Far East could hardly be more complete. At the close of the session Lloyd George expressed his sympathy for China, but declared he must stand by the 1917 treaties, whereupon the weary Clemenceau roused himself to the point of adding that every word Lloyd George had said could be taken as his also.

With their case now so clearly won, the Japanese demanded immediate action. Two days after this conference a peremptory note was sent to the Council of Four demanding final agreement for the transfer to Japan of all Germany's rights in Shantung. "They are not bluffers," President Wilson confided to Ray Stannard Baker, "and they will go home unless we give them what they should not have."

He made one more attempt to persuade them to soften their demands. While it was now apparent that the United States could expect no support from either Great Britain or France, and that the possible consequences of refusing to ratify the transfer of Shantung would be wholly an American responsibility, the President thought he might at least obtain definite assurances that Japan, once being awarded German rights in this province, would then herself surrender them to China. His success was not exactly spectacular.

The Japanese did indeed agree to recognize China's sovereignty in Shantung, but at the same time they made it clear that they intended to retain the right to establish a Japanese concession at Tsingtao, and would insist upon reserving all the economic privileges which had been held by Germany. They would return the shell; they planned to keep the kernel. Nor was there any understanding, as Wilson was later forced to admit before the Senate Committee on Foreign Relations, as to when any surrender of control over Shantung would be made. "That was left undecided," the President confessed, "but we were assured at the time that it would be as soon as possible."

With this vague promise Wilson had to be content. The text of the pertinent articles of the Versailles Treaty was duly agreed upon, and Japan was awarded complete and unconditional title to the leased territory; the railways, mines, and submarine cables, and all other economic concessions Germany had previously held in Shantung.

The controversy had naturally aroused widespread interest in the United States, and to President Wilson now fell the uncongenial task of putting as favorable an interpretation as possible on a signal defeat not only for American diplomacy in the Orient but for his general program at Versailles. His own idea was that the settlement was the "best that could be had out of a dirty past," but this could hardly be said publicly. The formal announcement of the agreement—if agreement it could be called—consequently stressed the importance of

Japan's promise eventually to return Shantung, and the limitations of any privileges she might still retain to those of an economic concessionaire. The President also stated, upon what evidence was not made clear, that there seemed to be a disposition upon the part of all the Powers to take up at an early date the possible abrogation of all spheres of influence in China. "I regard the assurances given by Japan," he concluded somewhat lamely, "as very satisfactory in view of the complicated circumstances."

Among the members of the American Delegation at Versailles, there was general regret at the course events had taken, but some difference of opinion as to the significance of Japan's victory. The optimistic and credulous Colonel House still thought all was for the best. He did not consider the Shantung issue very important; he was quite ready to trust the Japanese. Secretary Lansing, however, was very unhappy over it all. He had far more understanding of what was happening in the Far East. He later wrote that China had been offered up "as a sacrifice to propitiate the threatening Moloch of Japan," and he strongly resented the President's surrender to "a species of blackmail." Whatever the repercussions at home or in Europe, he said, we had sacrificed "our prestige in the Far East for a 'mess of pottage'— and a mess it is."

Wilson justified his course as necessary to save the League of Nations. He had been convinced that Japan was not bluffing in her threat to walk out of the peace conference. With Italy already withdrawn, this would have meant the end of his international organization. He foresaw a return to the old balance of power with

Germany, Russia, and Japan springing up to challenge the United States, Great Britain, and France. There would be no peace founded on justice and no new world order. The fate of Shantung, the sacrifice of principle involved, could not possibly bulk as large in his mind as this grave danger to the future rôle he believed the League was destined to play in safeguarding peace.

It is useless to conjecture on what might have happened had President Wilson insisted upon the immediate and unqualified return of Shantung to China. It might have brought on even more dangerous consequences than those which the President himself foresaw. The military party was strongly entrenched in Tokyo; it demanded a firm policy at Versailles. Japan might not only have withdrawn from the peace conference, but she might have asserted even more belligerently her right to retain the principal prize for which she had entered the war.

Wilson was concerned over what might happen in Europe rather than in Asia. Nevertheless, his surrender on this issue was in line with the general hands-off policy he had been pursuing in the Far East, without always fully realizing its implications, ever since his Administration had come into power. To have acted otherwise at this time, moreover, might have provoked Japan to anticipate the action she finally took twelve years later.

As it was, public opinion in this country immediately made Japan the object of vehement attack. A feeling of tension developed in American-Japanese relations which continued until the Washington Conference. While from China came angry complaints that all pledges for maintenance of the Open Door were now worth just that many scraps of paper, at home newspapers of all shades of opinion united in condemning our surrender to "Prussianized Japan."

The Twenty-One Demands, the secret treaties with the Allies, the Lansing-Ishii Agreement, and the Shantung settlement were termed successive steps in that aggressive program of imperialistic expansion which was making Japan the mistress of the East. She had taken advantage of the West's hour of need to assert so complete a domination over China that the Open Door no longer appeared to have any significance or reality.

"The blackest page in all our history," was Senator Hiram Johnson's characterization of the surrender on Shantung; the Hearst papers leaped into the fray to assail with renewed bitterness "wily, tricky, fight-thirsty Japan"; the usually moderate Boston *Transcript* spoke of "insolent and Hunlike spoliation"; and the New York *Call* described the transaction as "one of the most shameless deeds in the record of imperialistic diplomacy."

"Japan is steeped in German ideas," Senator Lodge told the Senate, "and regards war as an industry because from war she has secured all the extensions of her Empire. . . . She means to exploit China and build herself up until she becomes a power formidable to all the world. It is not merely that she will close the markets of China and obtain commercial and economic advantages. . . . Japan will be enabled to construct in that way a power which will threaten the safety of the world. . . . But the country that she would menace most would be our own, and unless we carefully maintain a very superior navy in the Pacific, the day will come when the United States will take the place of France in another great war to preserve civilization."

All the latent hostility in our attitude toward Japan, temporarily subdued in the comradeship of war, was aroused by this conviction that imperialism again held sway in the Far East.

CHAPTER IX

SIBERIA

AT THE SAME TIME THAT JAPAN WAS FIGHTING HER winning battle on the diplomatic front at Versailles, a confused and complicated situation in Eastern Asia was giving her militarists still further opportunity to extend their country's power on the mainland. It arose from what was one of the most fantastic developments of the late war period—Allied intervention in Siberia in the summer of 1918.

To disentangle even the principal threads of this involved story is almost impossible. The dramatic march of the lost legions of the Czecho-Slovaks across the Russian steppes and their bitter warfare against the Reds in the foothills of the Urals; the landing of Allied troops in Vladivostok; the factional fights between bands of Red and White partisans along the Amur; the rise and fall of the Kolchak dictatorship at Omsk; the lurid careers of the Cossack chieftains Semenov and Kalmikov who swept over Siberia in raids marked by a bloody trail of theft, rapine, and murder; the final débâcle of the Whites when the Bolsheviki drove eastward and the Allies withdrew completely discomfited—all this provided a kaleidoscopic series of events which today appears completely divorced from all reality.

The only consistent policy followed by the various factions involved in this struggle over Siberia was that of Japan. Although it was doomed to failure, Tokyo pursued a definite program which had as its apparent objective the establishment of a new sphere of influence in Siberia comparable to that set up in Manchuria and Shantung. Not until after the Washington Conference in 1921 was this attempt of the militarists to transform the Maritime Province of Siberia into a Japanese protectorate or a controlled buffer state finally abandoned.

The idea of intervention in Siberia had first been suggested by Japan in the summer of 1917 on the pretext that the revolution in Russia made some such step necessary to protect Allied interests in that part of the world. Just how this was to be done was never made wholly clear, but the Tokyo Government was prepared to act if the Allies approved its project. Fearful of the possible consequences in the already unsettled conditions of the Far East, the United States refused its sanction.

With the conclusion by Russia and Germany of the peace treaty of Brest-Litovsk, however, additional reasons could be advanced in favor of intervention. There were some two hundred thousand German and Austrian prisoners of war in Siberia who had been freed by the Bolsheviki and who might easily seize the vast stores of munitions and equipment which had been collected at Vladivostok. The Czecho-Slovaks, deserters from Austrian armies who had been fighting with the Russians, now needed assistance in their attempt to escape from Russia and reach the Western front. Allied assistance for the Whites might conceivably enable them to overthrow the Bolshevik régime and bring Russia back into the war. In view of these circumstances, President Wilson was strongly urged to reconsider his previous decision.

It placed him in a difficult quandary. "I have been sweating blood over the question of what is right and feasible to do in Russia," he wrote Colonel House in July, 1918. "It goes to pieces like quicksilver under my touch. . . ." He was afraid that once the Japanese disembarked their troops in the Maritime Province, they would refuse to withdraw them. But with the Tokyo Government playing upon France's desire for the creation of a military diversion on the Eastern front, and popular opinion becoming excited over the dangerous position of the Czecho-Slovaks, the pressure grew too strong for him to resist it. He was very much "fretted" with the Japanese attitude, the sympathetic Colonel House noted, but after a cable from Balfour saying that Japan was preparing to intervene on her own account and would resent the refusal of an Allied mandate to preserve order, the harassed President fell in line.

He officially proposed joint Allied intervention, in which such contingents as Japan dispatched to Siberia would be supplemented by forces representing America and the Allies, and he made it explicitly clear that it was an emergency measure which had no ulterior motives. The objects of the intervention, President Wilson said, were twofold: to aid the Czecho-Slovaks against the German and Austrian war prisoners, and to help the Russian people, wherever they sought such aid, in their efforts at self-government and self-defense. Under no condition was there to be any interference with Russia's political sovereignty or impairment of her territory. In conclusion, the President pointedly expressed the hope that Japan would make a similar declaration of policy.

She did so promptly. Whatever ambitions may have been flitting through the heads of her military leaders, the Tokyo Government reaffirmed its "avowed policy of respecting the territorial integrity of Russia and of abstaining from all interference in her internal politics." It further stated that as soon as the declared objects of intervention were achieved, the Japanese troops would be withdrawn.

On this understanding, and with the further one that the American and Japanese expeditionary forces should be equal in number, intervention became an actuality with the arrival at Vladivostok, in August, 1918, of the first contingents of Allied troops. But almost at once there was evidence that Japan was viewing the expedition in a somewhat different light than America. Instead of the seven or eight thousand troops Japan was expected to send, her force rapidly swelled to seventy thousand. The Japanese installed themselves not only in Vladivostok, but at Chita, Manchouli, and Nikolaevsk; at every point the Allied troops were heavily outnumbered, and the ranking officer was invariably a Japanese. "By October," one American observer wrote, "Japan had Siberia and Manchuria entirely under her power."

The Siberians and the Russians had no doubt of the motives which inspired Japan. They were convinced that her troops came as conquerors, not as friends, and that regardless of all protestations to the contrary, they sought permanent retention of the coastline. "The imperialists of Japan," *Izvestia,* official organ of the new

Soviet Government wrote, "want to check the Russian Revolution and cut off Russia from the Pacific. They want to grab the rich territory of Siberia and enslave Siberian workmen and peasants."

There was certainly a marked difference between the activities of the Japanese and American troops in Siberia. Under the command of General William S. Graves, the latter went strictly about what they conceived to be their business: maintaining order in Vladivostok, safeguarding the railroads, and observing a careful neutrality in Siberia's internal quarrels. Americans actually did very little, one army officer wrote, "but talk, nurse the railroads, distribute pamphlets and show pictures to prove to the Russians what a great nation we were—at home."

The Japanese, on the other hand, acted with dispatch and efficiency to set up a measure of control over Siberia which would in effect make them masters of the territory. Open support was afforded the Cossack chieftain, Ataman Semenov, although he had little claim to any real political standing and was actually interfering with the railroads the Allies were trying to keep open. Aid was extended to the still more notorious Kalmikov whose atrocities and murders completely discredited him in American eyes. In almost every respect, Japan was working at cross-purposes from the other members of the Allied expedition. Only the strictest discipline kept the recurring friction between the various forces from developing into open conflict.

Under these circumstances, conditions in Siberia grew more and more chaotic. The conclusion of peace made the Allies' position still more ambiguous and internal strife increased rather than diminished. Toward the end of 1919, affairs drew to a crisis. The Allies were unable to agree on a proposed advance against the Bolsheviki, and such order as had been maintained in the Eastern provinces quickly began to disintegrate.

The disgruntled Czechs began to fall back before the Red army, losing interest in a quarrel which was none of their direct concern, and the White Russians defending Omsk under Admiral Kolchak became panic-stricken. They had lost the support of the Siberian people, incensed by an unprincipled régime of oppression, brutality, and tyranny, and the government which was to have saved Russia from Bolshevism collapsed like a house of cards. Omsk fell into the hands of the Reds to the cheers of a populace which welcomed them as deliverers from the White terror.

The Allies were at last forced to recognize that they had achieved nothing whatsoever through intervention. Its sole result had been the delivery of Siberia to the Bolsheviki at the cost of incredible hardship and suffering on the part of the Siberian peasantry, inevitable victims of the partisan strife in which Reds and Whites alike preyed mercilessly upon the countryside. The futility of the whole undertaking had to be admitted.

Preparations were consequently made for complete Allied withdrawal, and by April 1, 1920, the greater part of the expeditionary forces, including all the Americans, had left Siberia. But the Japanese remained. Continued occupation of the Maritime Province, they stated, was imperative in their case because of the danger to Manchuria and Korea in the threat of revolutionary disturbances and the spread of Bolshevism.

Nor was the course of action to be followed by the Japanese military, freed of any restraining influence in Siberia itself, left long in doubt. Three days after the final withdrawal of the other Allied troops, surprise attacks against the pro-Bolshevik government were launched at Vladivostok, Nikolsk, and Habarovsk. The Russians were forced to conclude a new agreement which in effect gave Japan full control of the Siberian coastline. Within another month the massacre of some hundred and thirty Japanese by a band of Red partisans at Nikolaevsk was made the excuse for seizing the Northern half of the island of Sakhalin, withheld prize of the Russo-Japanese War.

The Japanese now controlled the entire Maritime Province. The government at Vladivostok was in their power. While further inland the pro-Bolsheviki had established a new government at Chita, which was to evolve into the Far Eastern Republic, their efforts to bring further territory under their influence met at every turn Japan's determined resistance. In Tokyo there was resentment over the needless waste of money and loss of life which intervention in Siberia had caused, but the military stubbornly refused to withdraw. Throughout 1920 and 1921 they zealously clung to their ambition to maintain Eastern Siberia as a Japanese protectorate.

During both the period of Allied intervention and the two following years, the United States strongly opposed Japan's aggressive policy and consistently protested against each new encroachment. For while America had assumed no obligation to uphold the Open Door in Siberia or to defend Russian territorial integrity, Japanese expansion in the North appeared to hold out the same ultimate threat to our interests in the Far East as expansion in Manchuria or Shantung. Siberia became in these years a new and dangerous manifestation of the underlying conflict between America and Japan in the Pacific area.

A first protest had been made when Japan dispatched such a large body of troops to Siberia in open violation of her previous pledge to send no greater a contingent than the United States. Possibly Secretary Lansing recalled regretfully the virtual free hand he had formerly accorded Japan in Manchuria when, in November, 1919, he summoned Viscount Ishii, now Ambassador at Washington, to explain what the American press, if not the State Department, was vigorously attacking as a new outbreak of Japanese imperialism. On this occasion, in any event, there was no compromise on "special interests." Lansing insisted that Japan live up to her agreements.

For a time there was an ominous calm in both Washington and Tokyo as a result of this open clash between the two Governments. The military party in Japan had no desire to back down before American protests; the Wilson Administration could make no further concessions so soon after its humiliating surrender on Shantung. But fortunately it was Tokyo which this time reconsidered. The more liberal element in the country forced through the recall of half the troops then in Siberia.

Japan was prepared to go hand-in-hand with America, Premier Hara told the press correspondents in Tokyo, strongly reiterating that his country had "absolutely no territorial ambitions in Siberia, will not take a single square foot of territory." Nevertheless, he seized the opportunity to point out that Japan was in a somewhat different position from the other participants in intervention. She necessarily had special interests in Siberia, he said, and could not afford to neglect any means of national self-defense until the Red menace was entirely averted.

The United States also resented Japan's flirtations with the Cossack adventurers Semenov and Kalmikov, roundly denounced by General Graves as bandits and murderers, and the intrigues over control of the Manchurian and Siberian railroads which found Japan counteracting the efforts of an American mission to bring some order out of the existing chaos.

For a time these protests were restrained because of the fear of Communism which swept over the world in 1919 and 1920. Japan's claim that the basis for her operations in Siberia was defense against the Reds awoke in some quarters a sympathetic response, largely induced by the hysterical alarms which Bolshevism then inspired. The dangers of Oriental imperialism seemed less menacing for the moment than those of Communist world revolution, and by the ultraconservatives Japan was judged to be fighting the battle of civilization against the perfidious Slav somewhat as she had in 1904.

The occupation of Sakhalin in 1920 could hardly be condoned on any such theory. Seizure of the northern half of this island was not necessary for the defense of Japan, let alone that of the Western World. The United States consequently protested against this move promptly and vigorously. Whatever the provocation, the American note pointed out, there did not appear to be any valid grounds for retaliation through territorial aggrandizement.

The Japanese Government found itself in a difficult position. Its hands forced by the military to defend and attempt to explain actions in Siberia for which it was not itself directly responsible, a situation arose not unlike that which was to develop some ten years later. The Foreign Office proposed; the War Office disposed. But in 1920 and 1921, there was a far stronger under-current of popular dissatisfaction with the Siberian adventure than there was in 1931 with the Manchurian adventure. It was strongly expressed in the Diet and would have been in the press, had not the Government rigorously censored it.

Among others, Viscount Kato, author of the Twenty-One Demands, took occasion to declare that intervention had been a complete failure, and that there was no reason for the continued occupation of the Maritime Province. Premier Hara defended it as best he could, but he was compelled to admit that the spread of Communism afforded no adequate grounds for Japanese policy.

The reply of the Tokyo Government to American protests consequently disclaimed any intent to hold Russian territory permanently, and promised withdrawal of the troops from Sakhalin and the coastline as soon as circumstances permitted. But the Foreign Office could not make good its pledges. The troops stayed on and there was no indication of their recall. When America protested still again, pointing out that continued occupation increased rather than allayed the unrest in Siberia, Japan merely repeated the now familiar thesis that conditions justified her action, and that she would withdraw her troops as soon as possible.

"It must be frankly avowed," Secretary of State Hughes later declared at the Washington Conference in a masterpiece of understatement, "that this correspondence has not always disclosed an identity of views between the two governments."

In the meantime, reports from Americans in the Far East graphically pointed out that whatever the official attitude, Japan gave every indication of planning to remain in Siberia indefinitely. Writing in the *Nation* in October, 1921, Nathaniel Peffer gave a picture of the situation which expressed the prevalent opinion in the Far East: Japan was firmly and permanently entrenched in Siberia and had carved out for herself a new empire which she was not likely to surrender. New issues and new problems had been raised in the Orient, this observer stated, which the United States could not ignore.

More outspoken was the report of Sidney C. Graves, son of the commander of the American forces in Siberia. "Is Japan preparing for a war with America, and was her Siberian expedition the first important step toward the realization of a Pan-Oriental Plan calculated to make such a struggle possible and profitable?" he wrote in the May, 1921, issue of *Current History*. "I am not a jingoist, but twenty months' intimate contact with the problem, as a staff officer of the American expedition, convinces me that such is the case."

Whatever the real plans of the Japanese militarists,

and no matter to what extent they were opposed by the more liberal elements in Japan, the continued occupation of the Siberian coastline, so long after the other Powers had withdrawn, did indeed seem to speak for itself. In the American mind it was inevitably linked with the assertion of special rights and powers in Manchuria, and the retention of Shantung, as still further evidence of Japan's undertaking to establish dominant control over all of Eastern Asia.

CHAPTER X

GATHERING WAR CLOUDS

WITH JAPAN EMBARKED UPON A PROGRAM OF IM-
perialistic expansion which seemed to accept
almost no limits, the unknown element in the troubled
international relations of the Pacific, as 1920 gave way
to 1921 and the Administration of President Harding
came into office, was how far the United States might
go in attempting to obstruct Japanese policies. Heretofore our protests had never been supported by any indication that we were willing to back them up by force.
We had not taken even as strong a stand against Japanese aggression in China as we had against Russian
aggression prior to the Russo-Japanese War. But in the
face of Japan's new activities on the Asiatic mainland, there was evidence that America was more determined than she had ever been before that in some way
Japan should be restrained from completely upsetting
the balance of power in Eastern Asia.

Moreover, there had now developed a further and
even more dangerous source of rivalry between the two
nations. Both the United States and Japan were rapidly
expanding their navies. Alarmists on either shore of the
Pacific freely predicted that war would be the inevitable
outcome of this threatening expression of the underlying conflict in national policies.

"We have seen the eyes of the world turned to the

Pacific," President Harding was to state at the Washington Conference. "With Europe prostrate and penitent, none feared the likelihood of early conflict there. But the Pacific had its menaces, and they deeply concerned us."

His Administration soon indicated that it was prepared to maintain a firmer policy in the Orient than that which had been pursued by President Wilson. It may not have been adopted in full consciousness of all its implications. Certainly Mr. Harding himself, with vague ideas of an Association of Nations disturbing habits of thought more closely attuned to the exigencies of Ohio politics, had little idea of what was actually at stake in the Far East. Nevertheless, the retreat from Europe was counterbalanced by an advance in Asia. To reëstablish American influence and prestige in the Orient, Secretary Hughes took the first opportunity to reaffirm the Open Door policy in no uncertain terms. The whole-hearted support of the administration was pledged to this principle "traditionally regarded as fundamental, both to the interests of China itself and to the common interests of all powers in China." It was a pronouncement enthusiastically hailed by the somewhat partisan New York *Tribune* as indicative of "a return to the policy abandoned by Mr. Wilson."

To support this stand a navy strong enough to assure American supremacy in the Pacific appeared clearly in order, and there was widespread demand for continuation of the building program initiated during the World War. With Japan strengthening her naval forces as a natural corollary to her territorial expansion, no other course seemed possible. The situation was hardly a new one in international history. Great Britain and Germany, after all, had recently found themselves in somewhat the same predicament.

Both the American and Japanese naval programs which were being carried forward in 1921 had originally been adopted as a safeguard against the possible consequences of a German victory in the World War. That of the United States had been planned for completion in 1922, while Japan's extended over a period ending in 1927. American building had been interrupted, however, and the status of new construction in the two countries was roughly the same.

The total strength of the American navy was 779,173 tons, with an additional 842,109 tons authorized, while Japan had 340,596 tons in active service, an additional 328,460 tons authorized, and further plans were "projected" for 368,370 tons. On a theoretical basis, nothing would have been more simple than to bring further building to a halt. The German fleet was destroyed. The only navy in the world larger than that of either America or Japan was the British navy. But the two nations were now building against each other, and neither would take the initiative in curtailing its program.

The most alarming aspect of this situation was the extent to which increased naval armaments tended to intensify the dangers which they were supposed to obviate. To cajole a tax-burdened public into supporting the necessary appropriations, every effort was made in this country to magnify the Japanese menace. It therefore became that much more real in the popular mind. On the other side of the Pacific, advocates of a larger Japanese navy built up a potential American menace in much the same way. Starting from the groundwork laid by our resentment of Japanese imperialism in Asia, and by Japanese resentment of our obstructive tactics in the Far East and treatment of Japanese immigrants, naval rivalry induced a mutual hostility which unquestionably held the seeds of war, had some provocative act on the part of either nation created a real crisis.

There was, for instance, the famous Yap controversy which might conceivably have furnished the necessary spark. Seldom have newspaper head-line writers struggling over foreign dispatches been granted such a boon as this expressive three-letter word. They made the most of it.

> Give us Yap! Give us Yap!
> The Yanks have put it
> The Yanks have put it
> The Yanks have put it
> On the map.

It would hardly be correct to imply that this song swept the country. But the popular demand grew that we hold on to our rights in Yap as a sign that there would somewhere be an end to Japanese imperialism.

Actually Yap was one of the former German islands—1,660 miles from Yokohama and 1,150 miles from Manila—which had been awarded Japan under a League of Nations mandate. Because of its possible importance as a cable station, we had refused to recognize this award, and one of the final acts of the Wilson Administration had been the dispatch of a note stating that the

United States would have to be consulted in regard to Yap's final disposition. Japan had brusquely refused to recognize our interests.

Secretary Hughes immediately took up the issue. Carefully phrased but unusually candid notes were periodically sent to Tokyo. The newspapers performed miracles of head-line exposition. Yap became a household word throughout the country. But neither nation budged from its original position. Of little importance in itself, the Yap issue loomed large on the Pacific horizon as a symbol of mounting tension between the rival Powers on either shore.

The underlying issue before the American people was said to be "whether or not the Japanese are to become the masters of the Pacific." The means to check Japanese aggression had to be provided at all costs. In no other way than by the creation of an all-powerful navy could America hope to block the ambitions of this Oriental Power "to expand its influence and usurp control throughout the Pacific." Books and magazine articles, as they had in earlier periods of tension, provided lurid pictures of the dangers to which America was exposed. *The Menace of Japan, The New Japanese Peril, Rising Japan, Must We Fight Japan?* and *The Next War* were titles expressive of the story being told the public.

The outcry was particularly vociferous on the West Coast which was as usual frantically engaged in expressing its anti-Japanese feeling through the adoption of further restrictions on Japanese residents. California had passed a new and more severe land law—a ballot-box ultimatum for war, the New York *World* declared —and the feeling engendered by this move was running high. The irate Californians angrily denied that they were in any way fomenting international discord. They dismissed Japanese protests on this local issue as a smoke screen to cover up their nefarious designs in Eastern Asia. "They are seeking to put the United States in a position of selfishness," one writer stated in an article syndicated throughout the country, "as a means of extorting the right to be selfish and imperialistic on their side."

Senator Phelan discovered the menace of Japan to be threatening not only the United States but the entire world. He pictured California in the rôle of Sobieski at Vienna, Charles Martel at Tours, and the Greeks at Marathon, valorously attempting to stem the tide of Oriental invasion.

A nation-wide symposium was held by Cornelius Vanderbilt, Jr., on whether the issues between America and Japan should be settled by negotiation or by the "arbitrament of the sword." And while he elicited scattered protests, as that of the Montana editor who told him "we are sick and tired of wasting our time on the numerous bogies created by you and your kind," the majority of responses indicated that the situation was generally viewed as extremely grave. At Washington it was at least considered serious enough to force the Cabinet, in March, 1921, to discuss the advisability of transferring the entire American fleet to the Pacific.

Public opinion in Japan was at the same time aroused to a high pitch of excitement by the jingoistic elements in that country. The racial discrimination of the California land laws, touching upon the sore point of national honor, and American attacks on Japanese imperialism were bitterly resented. The press characterized the United States as the actual aggressor in the Orient, and as an enemy to world peace hiding behind a false chivalry. Our real objective was stated to be control of the Pacific regardless of the rights of other nations. The Tokyo *Yorodzy* said that the United States—"no longer a country of Lincoln, but a land of selfish devils"—was trying to subject the entire world to its selfish program. "This action," it concluded, "is more harmful to the cause of humanity than was German militarism."

In a book which had a circulation of more than three hundred thousand copies, Ichiro Tokutomi caustically declared that the friendship of America had changed the moment it was discovered that Japan might possibly be a rival in the Pacific. "Not content to apply the Monroe Doctrine to both continents of North and South America," he wrote, "the United States seem to be bent on extending it to the continent of Asia. This is why America looks at Japan as constituting a menace to her." In Tokyo a public debate was held on the question "Shall Japan Fight America?" and in one newspaper a high army officer ran a series of articles on the American invasion of Japan.

The dangerous possibilities of this jingoistic furor were seen by those who most strenuously denied that there was any real cause for war. "If the present state of affairs is allowed to continue, no particular steps being taken to relieve the theoretical danger," wrote one Japanese, "war will be unavoidable." "So we talk war with Japan and Japan talks war with us," a speaker in the Senate declared, "and we drift along toward a war which would be the crime of all the centuries."

This feeling of impending conflict was not confined to the two countries most directly involved. Many foreign observers, recognizing the basic conflict in American and Japanese policy toward China, and interpreting our naval program as an answer to Japanese aggression, believed that hostilities could not long be postponed. European statesmen hinted cautiously of this new threat to world peace; the foreign press foresaw a conflict which might be as devastating as the World War.

In Great Britain it was generally agreed that rivalry for mastery of the Pacific was the crux of the so-called Far Eastern problem, and the naval expert, Hector Bywater, predicted a Japanese attack upon the United States in 1922. An Australian writer in the Brisbane *Courier* saw the United States as "the great barrier to Japanese ambitions." The Parisian journal *L'Œuvre* said that "the conflagration appears as fatally certain as lightning which leaps from two clouds charged with opposing currents."

If the alarmists could have had their way, these prophecies of war so current in 1920 and 1921 might well have materialized. But fortunately there was in both countries a concurrent movement to discover some other settlement than war for controversies so productive of ill-will. There was a growing popular resistance beneath the noisy outbursts of jingoists and big navy advocates to the dangerous course upon which America and Japan appeared to be embarked.

The World War was still too close at hand for another possible conflict to be viewed with any feeling but one of utter horror; its costs were still too heavy for taxpayers to bear with equanimity the expenditures which a new armaments race involved. There was strong opposition in Japan to ever mounting military and naval expenses, and an even greater revolt in this country. A settlement of our controversies with Japan was urged in order to bring to a halt the naval race they had inspired; a halt to the naval race was demanded to relieve the tension which made political settlements so difficult. Simultaneous, interrelated action was clearly needed whereby international faith and disarmament could be substituted for international distrust and big navies. Neither could be achieved without the other.

While the efforts of the liberals in Japan to modify foreign policy and bring about some reduction in armament expenditures could make little headway against the strong stand maintained by the military, the disarmament movement in this country attracted a greater following and was better able to exert its influence upon the Government. The idea of a naval holiday for Great Britain, the United States, and Japan was being discussed late in 1920, and as one of his last acts Secretary of the Navy Daniels suggested that a naval conference might well be called by the incoming Republican Administration.

With the introduction of the new naval appropriation bill, efforts were thereupon made for adoption of an amendment authorizing the President to call such a conference. They at first failed in the House but in the Senate received the powerful support of Senator Borah. His specific proposal was a conference of the three leading naval Powers to effect a reduction in their navies over a five-year period. On May 25, 1921, an amendment embodying this idea was adopted, and something like a month later the House concurred.

In the meantime the Administration had been considering the advisability of some such move and upon this expression of popular support prepared to act, although on very much broader lines than the Borah proposal. It had become convinced of the dangers of an armaments race on both political and economic grounds, and on July 8th Secretary Hughes instructed our Ambassadors to Great Britain, France, Italy, and Japan to "ascertain informally" whether the Governments to which they were accredited would consider participation in a general conference on the limitation of armament.

Before their replies could be received, a cable from our Ambassador in London, actually crossing his instructions from Washington, reported that Premier Lloyd George proposed to request that President Harding should call an international conference to consider all essential matters bearing upon the Far East and Pacific Ocean, and that he was about to make such a statement in the House of Commons. To forestall such a move, Secretary Hughes thereupon publicly announced, on July 11th, that the United States had addressed "informal but definite inquiries" to the Powers concerned for a conference on armament limitation and, in this respect following the lead of Lloyd George, added that it would also take up questions relating to the Far East. "It is manifest," the announcement of the Government's program stated, "that the question of limitation of armament has a close relationship to the Pacific and Far Eastern problems, and the

President has suggested . . . the consideration of all matters bearing upon their solution."

The explanation of the British Premier's impatient anxiety for a conference to settle Pacific problems is found in the fact that at just this time there was heated discussion in Great Britain over the possible lapse or renewal of the Anglo-Japanese Alliance, an issue which had aroused widespread concern both in England and in the Dominions.

First signed in 1902, and renewed in 1905 and in 1911, this alliance had originally been concluded to check possible Russian or German aggression in the Far East threatening the signatories' interests. It provided for mutual assistance should either Great Britain or Japan be attacked. In 1921 it had largely outlived its usefulness, due to the withdrawal of both Russia and Germany from Eastern Asia, and it was also widely felt that it was providing a protective shield for Japanese activities on the Asiatic mainland. The real problem its possible renewal presented, however, involved the obligations which it might impose upon Great Britain in the event of a Japanese-American war.

The United States, in any event, would have interpreted its continuance almost as a hostile act. In view of popular feeling toward Japan and the very real fear that war was not impossible, the alliance was regarded as affording aid and comfort to the enemy. Nor did Secretary Hughes hesitate to let the British Government know the views of the American Government.

Under the pressure of our opposition, and also that of the British Dominions, England was therefore anxious to allow the treaty to expire. But she had no wish to offend an old ally. Mutual agreement upon a new policy, and replacement of the old alliance by an accord in which America might be induced to participate, were consequently greatly desired. A Pacific conference held out for Great Britain the possibility of relief from the embarrassment caused by this difficult situation.

Immediate and unreserved approval of President Harding's suggestion on the part of the British Government was therefore a foregone conclusion. Japan had more reason to hesitate. It was to her interest to attempt to make what was from the Japanese point of view an entirely logical distinction between the naval and political issues at stake. While cordially welcoming the idea of negotiations for a limitation of armaments, Tokyo would have excluded from the conference "problems such as are of sole concern to certain particular Powers or such matters as may be regarded as accomplished facts."

There were no general outstanding problems in the Pacific for Japan. She held Shantung, Manchuria, and Siberia; she held the island of Yap. With international recognition of her position in the Far East, nothing would have been more acceptable than disarmament. Japan could not well bear the expense of her projected naval program and, in the long run, could not hope to compete successfully with America in any real outburst of naval rivalry. She wanted peace in the Pacific; she wanted it fully as much as did America. But the peace she wanted was based on the status quo in 1921, a status quo which indisputably made her supreme in Eastern Asia.

With equal logic, the United States felt that any disarmament should be dependent upon an adjustment, favorable to this country, of the issues raised by Japan's hold upon Manchuria, Shantung, and Siberia. The peace we sought was based upon a reversion to conditions prevailing before the war. The United States had modified the imperialism of 1900. We had in large part given up the old ambition for complete mastery of the Pacific. But our support of collective action in that part of the world was predicated upon international recognition of what we deemed our political and commercial rights. America demanded Japan's surrender of her wartime gains and the reëstablishment of the Open Door in China.

The issue between the United States and Japan was thus relatively simple. Japan had won control over a considerable part of Eastern Asia and thereby encroached upon certain American preserves, or, at least, territory which America was determined to keep out of Japan's exclusive control. We had the potential power—and were prepared to develop it—to force Japan to retreat somewhat as she had been forced to retreat in 1894. The Washington Conference was to attain these results without war. In the name of peace, Japan was to be coerced into guaranteeing a new international order in the Pacific for whose establishment she would have to make all the major sacrifices.

At no time has the United States taken a more decisive stand in support of its traditional policy in the Far East. Whether on this occasion we would have been prepared to use force in the event that Japan had refused to negotiate the issues at stake may be open to question, but we were at least willing to make a display of force. Our naval program was directly aimed at Japan. Unlike the situation prevailing during the war when the complications of intervention in the Far East forbade such action, we were free to exercise all the pressure at our command.

The American press made short shrift of Japanese objections to political discussion. Naturally Japan did not want her special position in the Pacific reviewed, declared the New York *American,* faithfully reflecting Mr. Hearst's persistent anti-Japanese attitude, because she was "a land and trade grabber and terrorizer of weaker people." The Baltimore *News* characterized her "strange hesitation" as an admission that she was "too determined to pursue her own line of action to waste time discussing it." Other papers pointed out that Japan always preferred separate negotiations in the hope of playing one Western nation off against another, and that she had no real sympathy for the collective system to which she had paid hypocritical lip-service by joining the League of Nations.

Any solution of the Pacific problem which fails "to puncture the Japanese claims to special interests in China," it was said in *Current Opinion,* "will but lay the foundation for the greatest military upheaval in history."

More sympathetic toward Japan was the New York *World,* which felt that it was only natural that she should be alarmed at a conference which was to take up her status as a great Power. "Japan has quite as good reason to distrust American motives," the *World* concluded, "as we have to distrust Japanese motives."

But it was not fashionable in 1921 to look upon international questions with any great degree of realism. To imply that "real equality of opportunity in the Far East almost inexorably means American supremacy," as Frank H. Simonds wrote, was to cast an unwarranted reflection on the generous idealism of American foreign policy. The New York *Tribune's* suggestion that since Japan was being called upon to surrender her claims in almost every controversy, she "might be placated for concessions on these points by agreement among the Powers to withdraw objection to her exploitation, say, of Manchuria," impugned our altruistic motives in up-holding the Open Door.

Dr. Nicholas Murray Butler, perhaps, best expressed the happy optimism of that day. He clearly recognized that disarmament in the Pacific depended upon political agreement. He further felt that such an agreement would have to provide "for the increasing population of Japan and its necessary economic expansion without involving exploitation of any other people, and without impairing the integrity of China or the maintenance there of the Open Door." To state the problem, how-ever, appeared virtually to solve it in the opinion of this learned internationalist. "It is not discreet," he added discreetly, "to say more just now than that some of the best-informed statesmen in Europe believe that such a formula can be found."

Throughout the world, except among the skeptical Japanese who advanced an Oriental version of our coup-let about the spider and the fly, the conference idea was taken up with great enthusiasm. With the replies to his original proposal universally favorable, notwithstanding Japan's reservations, President Harding consequently issued formal invitations for a conference to be held in Washington in November, and a cordial acceptance was promptly received in every case. In addition to Great Britain and Japan, the conference was to be attended by France, Italy, Belgium, the Netherlands, Portugal, and China.

The horrendous prophecies of war in the Pacific were now forgotten in the new wave of confidence in international negotiation. Political problems were to be discussed first; the Anglo-Japanese Alliance was to be supplanted by a new general agreement. Then arms limitation. It was all very simple. "If agreement on the problems of the Pacific can be reached," as the Richmond *News Leader* stated, "the question of disarmament will settle itself almost automatically."

With President Harding and Secretary Hughes exuding confidence, the European statesmen gorgeously optimistic, no happier atmosphere for an international conference could have been created. Even the Japanese felt compelled to fall in line. "Peace in the Pacific," Premier Hara told the New York *World,* "is the insistent cry of the Japanese people."

The stage was set. Peace and good-will were to be enthroned in a wicked world. A new conference had been called to redress the balance of the old. The world breathed easier as the war clouds in the Pacific faded away.

And curiously enough the conference was to achieve a measure of success which astounded the skeptics. The world was to make a nobler gesture toward disarmament than it ever had before; a new international order was to be established in the Pacific. Not for a full ten years was the world to realize that this imposing edifice had been built upon sand and that the triumphs of this peace were more apparent than real.

CHAPTER XI

WASHINGTON CONFERENCE

THE CONFERENCE ON THE LIMITATION OF ARMAMENT summoned by President Harding was formally opened in Washington on November 12, 1921. It was a proud occasion for the American people. Never before had such a distinguished assembly of foreign statesmen met in this country. The galleries were crowded as the delegations of the participating nations took their places. Secretary Hughes, cool and dignified, headed that of the United States; the suave and polished Balfour represented Great Britain; Premier Briand was to speak for France, and Prince Tokugawa for the Japanese delegation. For once the three hundred-odd newspaper correspondents could not refer to a Japanese envoy as an "inscrutable Oriental." The descendant of the shoguns was described as looking and acting "like a friendly, neighborly grocer in a smallish American town."

While the audience was interested and alert, no one expected any unusual development to mark this opening session; no one felt the imminence of what Mr. Balfour was later to characterize as "the inspired moment . . . on which all the greatness of this great transaction really depends." It was not until well along in Secretary Hughes's address as chairman of the Conference that his hearers suddenly realized that history was in the making. Then a wave of mingled admiration and astonishment swept over the assembly as the head of the American delegation stated in clear and explicit terms his program for naval disarmament. He gave actual tonnage figures. He announced the names not only of the capital ships his own country was prepared to dismantle, but those which he proposed Great Britain and Japan should scrap.

Here was a striking example of the new diplomacy. Secretary Hughes had laid his cards on the table, and his definite proposals were a challenge to action which could not be ignored. There is no question but that it was the big moment of the conference. By voicing so dramatically the world-wide demand for an end to naval rivalry, Secretary Hughes had taken an immense stride toward the successful conclusion of a disarmament treaty.

There was hardly any reference in this opening address to the political problems so intimately related to naval power and so important to any agreement for the limitations of arms. They were completely overshadowed by the drive to secure a naval treaty. One experienced commentator on the political scene complacently declared that "the questions of the Far East were not an essential part of that great adventure." But they were essential. Negotiations for their settlement proceeded simultaneously with those on the naval program. Had not what was then believed to be a lasting accord been reached on the points at issue between America and Japan, the naval treaty could not have been concluded.

The proposals for naval disarmament advanced by

Secretary Hughes, in any event, were so definite and concrete, and represented such practical savings for harassed taxpayers here and abroad, that public opinion generally hailed them with tremendous enthusiasm. This country was swept by a wave of crusading fervor which might well have forced our delegation to present them as America's ultimatum to the world. We were not so deeply concerned over the situation in the Far East, for all the alarms and excursions of the previous year, as to weigh any possible future risks of naval limitation against the immediate gains of so dramatic a gesture in the name of peace.

The American plan contemplated the complete abandonment by the naval Powers of their capital ship-building programs and a ten-year truce on all new construction. It went further than that. It proposed that the United States should at once undertake to scrap 845,740 tons of battle-ships either built or building, Great Britain 583,375 tons, and Japan 448,928 tons—an aggregate total for the three nations of 1,876,000 tons. The tonnage of the navies of these three nations, as estimated by American naval experts, would then be:

Great Britain ....604,450 tons
United States ....500,650 tons
Japan ....299,700 tons

After expiration of the ten-year truce, replacements would be allowed on the basis of an upper limit of 500,000 tons each for Great Britain and the United States, and 300,000 tons for Japan. Actual existing strength in capital ships was the measure for this drastic program of reduction. It was put forward by Secretary

Harris & Ewing

THE JAPANESE DELEGATION AT THE WASHINGTON CONFERENCE
Left to right: Baron Shidehara, Admiral Kato, Prince Tokugawa, Mr. Hanihara.

Hughes on the ground that any attempt to develop a ratio based on any other considerations would lead only to "profitless and interminable discussion."

This was the basic strength of the American program. Fourteen years later the grounds upon which the 5-5-3 ratio were based were conveniently forgotten by both the United States and Japan. Continuation of the superiority it accorded the American fleet over the Japanese fleet was defended on our part as necessary for national security, while for the same reason Japan demanded a higher ratio. The "profitless and interminable discussion" resulting from this debate on "equality of security" versus "equality of armaments" ended only with Japan's abrogation of the Washington treaty.

Great Britain and Japan at once accepted the general provisions of the Hughes program in 1921, the latter nation's reply stating that "gladly accepting . . . the proposal in principle, Japan is ready to proceed with determination to a sweeping reduction in her naval armament."

Full agreement was not quite as simple, however, as this official response would indicate. Japan was strongly in favor of naval limitation; the Japanese people no less than the American resented the huge bill they had to meet for naval expansion. But while the Japanese delegation had come to Washington knowing that it would have to accept, in the main, whatever proposals the United States put forward, there was one point on which it was prepared to insist.

In conjunction with this sweeping naval reduction Japan demanded an agreement barring any further construction of naval bases or fortifications in the three

Powers' insular possessions in the Pacific. For a time Japan also sought to better her relative capital ship position by a change from the 5-5-3 ratio to a 10-10-7 ratio, but in the face of Secretary Hughes's uncompromising opposition this issue was after a time dropped. Japan concentrated on barring naval bases.

Possible fortifications in the Philippines, at Guam, or in the Aleutian Islands, in view of their proximity to Japan, were considered a strategic advantage for the United States which could not be offset by any possible naval bases which Japan might develop. They might enable an American fleet to operate in Japanese waters, according to the naval theorists, while a Japanese fleet would under no circumstances be able to operate in American waters. From the point of view of security from attack and freedom of action in the Far East, the issue was a vital one.

By accepting an inferior naval ratio Japan was in so strong a position to insist upon this point that Great Britain and the United States could not hold out against it. Possibly no agreement could otherwise have been concluded. The naval treaty embodying the 5-5-3 ratio for the United States, Great Britain, and Japan, together with lower ratios for France and Italy, consequently stipulated that the existing status quo of Pacific naval bases should be preserved. The United States undertook not to fortify the Philippines, Guam, or the Aleutian Islands; Great Britain agreed not to develop any further her naval base at Hongkong; and Japan was pledged not to construct any new bases in her insular possessions.

With the failure of the Washington Conference to

apply the principle of naval limitation to auxiliary vessels, largely through the opposition of France, we are not here concerned. The Five Power Naval Treaty was its great achievement in the realm of disarmament and constituted a contribution to this cause, regardless of later developments, which will forever give the Washington Conference a special significance in history. The treaty represented a forward step which stood out in marked contrast—and was to continue to stand out in marked contrast—to the uncertain, wavering, and entirely inconclusive approach to disarmament on the part of the League of Nations.

Upon its conclusion naval experts of each of the three nations claimed that their country had made the greatest sacrifice to the common cause. Moreover, in each instance they could make out a strong case. Great Britain had peacefully surrendered her traditional naval supremacy, and for the first time in history accepted equality with another Power. America had agreed to scrap more tonnage than either other Power and had withdrawn from a race in which her greater resources would almost inevitably have made her the eventual victor. Japan had submissively accepted a ratio which gave her a fleet not much more than half as powerful as that of her American rival.

British Tories lamented that Britannia no longer ruled the waves; Mr. Hearst's press grieved over our sacrifices "for the painted rattle called Limitation of Armaments"; and a reactionary Tokyo paper cried aloud that no one could deny that "Japan has had her hands and feet cut off in Washington." Nevertheless, the general feeling in favor of disarmament was so

strong that the treaty was popularly hailed as being
more conducive to the maintenance of world peace than
any previous event in history.

"Probably no more significant treaty was ever signed,"
the American delegation declared in its report. "If naval
experts stand askance on the arms treaties," wrote a
Japanese historian, "mankind at large is overwhelm-
ingly gratified by the Washington achievement."

Ironically enough he added: "Let time prove which
is right."

Prior to the adoption of this treaty, and as a move
absolutely essential to its completion, the Conference
had taken up the problem presented by the Anglo-
Japanese Alliance. In view of our declared position that
its continuation "could not fail to be regarded as seriously prejudicial to our interests," its abrogation in
one way or another had been a foregone conclusion.
The difficulty lay in devising a substitute agreement
which would meet British objections to summarily
abandoning a wartime ally, and at the same time serve
as a possible check upon Japanese imperialism. This
meant American participation in some accord on terms
which would not conflict with our national prejudice
against entangling alliances.

The solution was found in the Four Power Treaty.
In this rather pallid and innocuous pact—"we have
discarded whisky and accepted water," Ambassador
Hanihara declared—the United States, Great Britain,
Japan, and France agreed to respect one another's insular possessions in the Pacific, and to consult together
should any development arise threatening the status quo

of these possessions. It allowed England and Japan gracefully to forget their old alliance; not much more could be said in its favor. There was no provision for any sort of action, either individually or collectively, in the event that any threatening circumstances should arise.

It fell to Senator Henry Cabot Lodge, fresh from his bitter attacks against American membership in the League of Nations, to announce American participation in this new accord. He took careful pains to emphasize its limitations. His speech was chiefly a glowing panegyric of the beauty and romance of the Pacific islands whose security it was supposed to guarantee:

> Sprinkled isles,
> Lily on lily that o'erlace the sea. . . .

But on a sterner note, with oblique reference to the iniquities of the League from which he had so narrowly saved America, he pointed out that "no military or naval sanction lurks anywhere in the background or under cover of these plain and direct clauses."

For all the innocuousness of its provisions, the treaty came in for vehement criticism. While political motives served to discount Senator Reed's attack on it as "treacherous, treasonable and damnable," the Washington *Herald* characterized it as "diplomatic language for a defensive alliance, no more, no less." The Socialist New York *Call* and Hearst's New York *American* found themselves in surprising agreement: the treaty was an alliance of imperialism.

The American delegation felt quite differently. "No greater step could be taken," it reported, "to secure the unimpeded influence of liberal opinion in promoting peace in the Pacific." But this clearly referred not so much to the Four Power Treaty as to the abrogation of the Anglo-Japanese Alliance. The belief that Japan would now be forced by the withdrawal of England's tacit support to pursue a more coöperative policy in the Orient found wide acceptance.

The third treaty concluded at the Washington Conference directly involved international policy toward China.

The status of that distracted country was recognized to be the crux of the entire Pacific problem. The misunderstandings and controversies in the Far East, our delegation report stated, "centered principally about China." The Japanese publicist, K. K. Kawakami, declared that if America and Japan should ever go to war, it would be "because of disagreement on the Chinese question." If the naval treaties were to endure, if there were to be reasonable hope of maintenance of the new status quo in the Pacific, a solution of this problem had to be found on terms acceptable to the three nations chiefly concerned: the United States, Japan, and China herself.

The American delegation, motivated by those two neatly coinciding objectives of protecting American trade interests and safeguarding China's independence, was more concerned, however, over clipping the wings of Japanese imperialism than in soberly considering whether there might be any possible justification for Japan's program of expansion on the Asiatic mainland. There was little disposition to consider such a possibility as that contained in the New York *Tribune's* suggestion that Japan might be placated for her other concessions by withdrawing objections to her exploitation of Manchuria.

To the end, therefore, of substantiating the Open Door policy as strongly as possible, four resolutions were introduced to the Conference which very fully embodied the historic American policy in the Orient. As finally adopted, for Japan had no recourse other than to accept a set of principles whose abstract justice none could deny, they committed the signatory Powers:

1. To respect the sovereignty, the independence, and the territorial and administrative integrity of China;

2. To provide the fullest and most unembarrassed opportunity to China to develop and maintain for herself an effective and stable government;

3. To use their influence for the purpose of effectually establishing and maintaining the principle of equal opportunity for the commerce and industry of all nations throughout the territory of China;

4. To refrain from taking advantage of conditions in China in order to seek special rights or privileges which would abridge the rights of subjects or citizens of friendly States, and from countenancing action inimical to the security of such States.

These resolutions were duly incorporated in the Nine Power Treaty, together with certain other provisions further designed to aid China, including a guarantee of her neutrality in the event of a war to which she was not a party, and the pact was signed by those nations having interests in the Far East: the United States, Great Britain, Japan, France, Italy, Belgium, the Netherlands, Portugal, and China herself. "It is be-

lieved that through this Treaty," the American delegation declared, "the Open Door in China has at last been
made a fact."

If a treaty, any more than an informal engagement,
could have such a decisive effect, the Open Door in
China had certainly become the fact so confidently proclaimed. It was now, for the first time, clearly written
into international law. But experience has again and
again proved that if an international agreement is to
have any reasonable expectations of permanence, it
must represent a settlement mutually satisfactory to the
contracting parties. This could not be said of the Nine
Power Treaty.

For the United States, it represented the final triumph of the policy which we had been pursuing ever
since Secretary Hay dispatched his first circular notes
to the Powers in 1899. Going back still further, it was
the culmination of the policy which had governed our
relations in the Far East since the opening of trade
with Canton. The maintenance of China's independence and full equality of commercial rights for all nations trading with China were now so fully guaranteed
that in the optimistic atmosphere of 1922 any further
disputes on these questions appeared impossible.

It is true that the new treaty accorded no special
privileges to the United States. But we had never sought
them. The superiority of our natural resources, industrial organization, and facilities for foreign trade were
believed, both in this country and by our commercial
rivals, to afford us, under conditions of equality, a
marked competitive advantage over any other nation.
Business interests felt confident of their ability to more

than hold their own in the Chinese market provided only they were allowed that fair field and no favor which Secretary Hay had sought two decades earlier. The Open Door, as Frank H. Simonds had said, inexorably meant American commercial supremacy. That is why we had adopted it as our policy.

For Japan, on the other hand, the Nine Power Treaty was a signal diplomatic defeat. It expressed in unmistakable terms the refusal of the Powers to recognize what she had persistently claimed to be her special position in China. The right to continental expansion which she advanced as a consequence of her own overcrowded condition and need for controlled sources of raw materials was summarily dismissed. Nor did Japan receive compensation in any other quarter to reconcile her to acceptance of a settlement of the Far Eastern problem which was wholly in accord with the American thesis and utterly at variance with her own.

Japan nevertheless had to sign the Nine Power Treaty since a political isolation which she was not then strong enough to risk, if not more drastic measures, would have been the immediate consequence of any hesitation. Refusal to acknowledge the Open Door would have been accepted as indisputable proof of aggressive designs against China. It would have been an admission of imperialistic ambitions. The potential naval and military strength of the United States, with the moral support of the other Powers, enabled this country to exert a measure of pressure against Japan which was none the less coercive for being applied in the name of peace.

At the same time Japan was compelled to make

further concessions, at least in principle, which served to implement the Nine Power Treaty. Through separate accords or public statements of policy written into the minutes of the Washington Conference, she surrendered on every one of the controversial issues which had necessitated the inclusion of Far Eastern questions in the conference agenda. She agreed to certain modifications in the special privileges she had heretofore claimed in Manchuria, officially withdrawing Group 5 of the Twenty-One Demands and giving up her preferential rights in the three Eastern provinces. She undertook to withdraw immediately the Japanese troops in Shantung, sell to China the former German-owned railroad, and abandon all special economic privileges in the province. In the special treaty embodying these concessions, stated the counsel of the Chinese delegation, it was "easily demonstrable that China has won an almost complete victory."

While Siberia had not been a subject of formal negotiation, Japan also specifically disclaimed any designs on Russian territory. In response to the pressure exerted by Secretary Hughes, she undertook not only to evacuate the coastline but to restore Sakhalin. And finally, in return for American recognition of her mandate over Yap, free access to the little island's cable facilities was conceded, and a further agreement made not to establish there either a naval or military base.

Here was retreat all along the line: formal renunciation of whatever ambitions she may have been harboring for further expansion in Eastern Asia. Once again Japan had been forced to disgorge wartime gains and had been repulsed on her course toward imperialistic aggrandizement. America had assumed the leadership in forcing this Japanese surrender through sponsoring a series of treaties which at one and the same time protected American interests and established the highest standards for the maintenance of peace and good-will in the Pacific.

When upon final conclusion of the Conference public opinion in this country attempted to interpret the net effect of the various accords which had been signed, a wide divergence of views made itself manifest. On the surface there appeared to be little question of the complete victory won by American diplomacy. Japan had agreed to our right to a navy almost twice as powerful as her own. The Anglo-Japanese Alliance had been scrapped, and an innocuous accord substituted for it which no longer assured Japan of British support should her policies get her into international difficulties. Formal acceptance of the Open Door policy guaranteed our free access to Chinese markets and apparently assured us that opportunity for trade expansion which had been the persistent dream of a century.

The American delegation happily accepted this general interpretation of the results of the Conference. The concessions made by Japan were considered fully to justify "the relation of confidence and good-will expressed in the Four Power Treaty and upon which the reduction of armament provided in the Naval Treaty may be contemplated with a sense of security." Japan was said to be out to imitate the best of the West as formerly she had imitated the worst. She had delighted her friends, it was stated, and disappointed her enemies.

On the other hand, serious question was raised as to the validity of these accords. It was pointed out that despite the solemnity of the engagements in which Japan had entered, there was no guarantee that she would abide by them. Recognizing the extent to which they represented a triumph for America and a defeat for Japan, it was pointedly asked on what grounds could it be believed that Japan would permanently honor her obligations. And from this point of view, the failure of the treaties to include any provision for their own enforcement was interpreted as transforming an apparent victory for American policy into a signal defeat in view of the effective naval supremacy Japan retained in the Western Pacific.

There was little reason to believe, wrote one commentator, that reiteration of a long line of promises would change the present position or prevent the future progress of the Japanese military machine. The Japanese had won a dramatic victory, Raymond Leslie Buell said, "due to their ready adherence to declarations 'in principle' which the Conference was forced to accept at their face value and in the sincerity of which the general public probably believed. . . . Peace at Washington was purchased at the sacrifice of the Open Door."

In somewhat the same way there was a division of opinion in Japan. While there was little disposition to acknowledge a Japanese victory, the more liberal elements believed that the sacrifices Japan had been compelled to make were compensated by the peace and security the Washington Conference appeared to guarantee.

"We realized that a new spirit of moral consciousness had come over the world," Admiral Kato declared, "but we could not bring ourselves truly to believe that it had struck so deeply into the souls of men until we came to Washington. . . . Japan is ready for the new order of thought—the spirit of international friendship and coöperation for the greater good of humanity—which the Conference has brought about."

At the same time, there was strong popular resentment against those consequences of the accords which reflected Japan's surrender of her wartime gains. "Hateful and haughty America" was bitterly attacked in the reactionary press for enforcing upon Japan "a peace without liberty, a slavish peace." One paper stated that "the preposterous sacrifices and concessions made by Japan have furnished the United States and Britain with unexpectedly great successes and satisfaction, diplomatically and strategically"; another that Japan had "sustained such a loss as she would have suffered had she been defeated in her desperate war with Russia."

Mass meetings were held in Tokyo which assailed the injustice of the American attitude and excoriated the Japanese delegates to the Conference for signing treaties so inimical to their country's real interest. At one of these meetings, organized by the National Young Men's Association on American Issues, an army officer solemnly warned that it would be well to wait some ten years before becoming jubilant over the prospects of peace in the Pacific.

In substance, the value of the Washington accords as a whole depended entirely upon Japan's good faith. If they had been signed solely because Japan had been coerced into surrender, as she had been in 1894, and their repudiation awaited only the development of sufficient strength to abrogate them with impunity, the victory for American policy was entirely illusory. For the limitation upon naval construction and the agreement whereby we could not fortify our naval bases clearly enough afforded Japan a potentially stronger position in the Western Pacific than she had ever had before.

But in 1922 there appeared little reason to doubt Japan's good faith, and despite subsequent events, the assumption that she did not intend to abide by her obligations would not appear wholly justified. For while no Japanese Government could forswear the basic objectives of national policy in regard to Asiatic supremacy, the aggressive program followed during the World War —in China and in Siberia—had aroused widespread popular opposition, and a more moderate policy was being advocated by the liberal elements within Japan. For them the Washington Conference represented an opportunity to wrest control of foreign policy from the militarists and, in conformity with the new treaties, seek to promote Japan's interests in a spirit of international coöperation.

If Japan had no other alternative than to accept the settlement of Pacific problems forced upon her by the United States, Admiral Kato was nevertheless expressing a feeling widely held by Japanese liberals when he spoke of Japan's readiness to welcome the new order. They were prepared to accept the spirit of international friendship which in 1922 was winning so strong a hold upon both nations and statesmen throughout the world.

It is now easy to recognize, however, that the change was too drastic a one to be enduring in view of the failure of Japan to obtain any concessions in exchange for those she had been constrained to make. The military and reactionary groups could not accept this full retreat from the Asiatic mainland. While temporarily unable to make their views prevail, they did, indeed, harbor their strength for a renewal of the offensive when times were more propitious. They fell back upon the old advice of Japanese statesmen to wait until the West was too involved in its own affairs to be free to block Japanese ambitions.

The tragic mistake of the Washington Conference was that its participants banked too heavily upon the continuation in power of Japanese liberalism, and at the same time weakened the position of the liberals by refusing to afford any recognition to Japan's historic aspirations. Regardless of their validity from a moral point of view, these ambitions had become too much a part of national tradition to be cast aside so easily. It is possible that if the problems centering upon the status of China had been decided upon a more realistic basis, if in some form Japan's special interests in Manchuria had been acknowledged, the Washington accords would have had greater permanency.

The only other way in which their continued observance by Japan could have been guaranteed would have been by some joint international undertaking for their enforcement. But the United States trusted to moral force for the maintenance of the status quo in the Pacific, and we gave up the right to have either the fleet or the naval bases which might have enabled us to prevent any recrudescence of Japanese imperialism. We had won a significant diplomatic victory, refused to make any real concessions, and relied upon international good-will to maintain this American-made peace. Granted the strength of Japanese ambitions and the pressure of economic imperialism, the Washington accords contained the elements of their own collapse.

American public opinion, nevertheless, was ready to accept the results of the Conference at their face value. The wish was father to the thought: an enduring peace had been established. Armament limitation was itself interpreted as signal proof of the new international order. Its disintegration could not be envisaged when the new spirit of conciliation was contrasted with the distrust and suspicion of the previous year.

The naval treaties had brought about "the miracle of disarmament," the New York *Globe* declared, and represented "the first gain from the World War, the first crop from the gigantic planting of dead men's bones and vast watering with blood." The Cleveland *Plain Dealer* said that the Four Power Treaty had made it inconceivable that "Japan and the United States could even approach the brink of war." Through the Nine Power Treaty, in the opinion of the New York *World*, "the threatening questions of the Pacific and the Far East have been removed from the category of war breeders."

It was in this triumphant spirit that President Harding officially brought the sessions of the Washington Conference to a close. All doubts were resolved, all misgivings forgotten. It was the "beginning of a new and better epoch in human progress." The indictment of national dishonor had been drawn, and the world was prepared "to proclaim the odiousness of perfidy or infamy." Through conference and negotiation it had at last been learned "how alike, indeed, and how easily reconcilable, are our national aspirations; how sane and simple and satisfying to seek the relationships of peace and security."

"It is all so fine, so gratifying, so reassuring, so full of promise," the President declared amid prolonged applause which must today echo somewhat hollowly, "that above the murmurings of a world sorrow not yet silenced; above the groans which come of excessive burdens not yet lifted but soon to be lightened; above the discouragements of a world yet struggling to find itself after surpassing upheaval, there is the note of rejoicing which is not alone ours or yours, or of all of us, but comes from the hearts of men of all the world."

CHAPTER XII

ERA OF GOOD FEELING

FOR ALMOST TEN YEARS FOLLOWING THE WASHINGTON Conference, its high promise for peace and security in the Pacific appeared to be realized. During the critical period which saw civil war and antiforeign feeling at their height in China, the Powers generally acted in concert and abided by the obligations they had assumed in the Nine Power Treaty. Even the "positive policy" followed for a time by Japan did not have any immediate serious consequences. If there were occasional discordant notes in the symphony of international good-will, notably the acrimonious controversy springing from the Japanese exclusion act passed in 1924, relations between the United States and Japan were generally characterized, between 1921 and 1931, by a cordiality which the statesmen of the two countries lost no occasion to emphasize and cultivate.

Developments immediately after the Conference afforded every reason to believe that Japan had turned her back upon imperialism and fully intended to live up to both the letter and the spirit of the Washington accords. Under the premiership of Admiral Baron Kato a policy of fulfilment was loyally followed. Japan promptly began to scrap those capital ships whose abandonment was required by the naval treaty, proceeded to the successful negotiation with China of the final

terms for the return of Shantung, and at last undertook the effective evacuation of Siberia.

As indicative of a more conciliatory policy toward
China and acceptance of the principles underlying the
Nine Power Treaty, the further step was taken of abrogating the ambiguous Lansing-Ishii Agreement. Our
vague recognition of Japan's special interests in Manchuria was nullified through a formal exchange of notes.
The American and Japanese Governments succinctly
stated that "in the light of the understanding arrived
at by the Washington Conference," the correspondence
between Lansing and Viscount Ishii in 1917 would
be considered cancelled and "of no further force or
effect."

Through these successive moves the atmosphere of
hostility which had hung so heavily over American-
Japanese relations prior to the Conference completely
cleared. In a score of different ways it was made plain
that now all was peace and good-will. News articles and
magazine discussions of Japanese policy no longer
warned ominously of gathering war clouds and the in-
evitability of conflict in the Pacific. "Japan Keeps
Faith," "Japan's New Policy of Conciliation," and
"Japan's New Diplomatic Path" set the tone of American comment on the changing scene in the Far East.

There were still occasional observers to point out that
friction between the United States and Japan, with
China the helpless cause, could hardly be avoided from
time to time. Skeptics doubted if the leopard could so
completely—or at least permanently—change his spots.
At least one Japanese commentator definitely stated
that the new policy of peace and conciliation toward

China will depend much on the rise or fall of the liberal movement in Japan." But it was generally assumed that liberalism in Japan was now too strong to be overthrown, and that the nation was permanently dedicated to the collective responsibility for peace which was the foundation of the new international order in world affairs.

The frank recognition on the part of many Japanese spokesmen that between 1914 and 1921 their country had pursued an aggressive and imperialistic policy fortified foreign confidence in their further statements that this was now all a thing of the past. Moreover, the new policy appeared to be the logical consequence of existing circumstances.

As critical a commentator as Raymond Leslie Buell felt compelled to retract certain of the views he had so forcibly expressed in 1922. Commenting on his own book on the Washington Conference, he declared that he had underestimated "the moral forces resulting from that conference which changed Japan's Oriental policy." Another well-informed authority wrote in *Foreign Affairs* that Japan had associated herself with the international policy of fair dealing not as a diplomatic gesture, but as a result of a carefully considered dictate of enlightened self-interest. In going even beyond the terms of the Washington accords, the Tokyo Government had thus "restored confidence in the good faith and the good-will of Japan."

Among many other Americans, Franklin Delano Roosevelt welcomed this new Japan to the comity of nations. Pointing out that she had returned Shantung, evacuated Siberia, and was scrapping her condemned capital ships faster than was the United States, the future President declared in an article in the magazine *Asia* in 1923 that Japan had demonstrated her desire "to prove to the world that suspicions of the past are no longer justified." In turn he would have had America make some gesture to prove that this new policy was being accepted in like spirit. He proposed that we might well recognize in some form the real necessity to Japan of the markets and raw materials of Manchuria, and on this basis seek out her further aid in our own great task of establishing a new international order.

"Why, in all reason," Mr. Roosevelt asked, "should not Japan, shoulder to shoulder with us, provide her aid as well? If instead of looking for causes of offense, we in all good faith confidently expect from Japan co-operation in world upbuilding, we shall go far toward insuring peace."

International friendships, however, are subject to the whims of popular passion; they are at the mercy of any provocative incident. American-Japanese relations were sorely strained by the 1924 Immigration Law, and only the exercise of moderation on either side of the Pacific forestalled a serious crisis. Just as the sudden suspicion of Japan's motives in Manchuria, intensified by the anti-Japanese feeling fostered by the San Francisco school-board incident, had poisoned the friendship so enthusiastically proclaimed during the Russo-Japanese War; just as Japanese aggression in Shantung and Siberia had undermined the World War entente, so did this new controversy break in upon the harmony of these halcyon days which followed the Washington Conference.

The terms of the Immigration Law expressly barred from entry into the United States "aliens who are ineligible for citizenship." And aliens ineligible for citizenship expressly meant Orientals. There was little validity to claims that such a law violated any treaty we had with Japan. None could dispute the right of the United States to legislate as it chose on a question of wholly domestic concern. Nevertheless, this provision of the law was directly aimed at the immigration of Japanese. It constituted an act of discrimination against the nationals of a friendly nation which could hardly be justified on any higher grounds than those of selfish expediencey.

It was adopted largely at the instigation of the anti-Japanese elements in California and represented the culmination of the campaign they had been waging for effective restriction of Japanese immigrants since the beginning of the century. For this issue had not been permanently settled by the Gentlemen's Agreement of 1908 whereby Japan herself undertook to refuse passports to laborers desiring to enter the United States. California had never been satisfied with this settlement. The persistent agitation against any Japanese immigration had continued.

This attitude prevailed, moreover, despite the very definitely conciliatory policy in regard to immigration maintained by the Japanese Government throughout this period. It had faithfully lived up to its obligations under the Gentlemen's Agreement. It had met the "picture bride" issue by withdrawing passport privileges for the entry of laborers' wives. It had closely co-operated with the American authorities at every turn.

The effectiveness of this policy, from the American point of view, was graphically illustrated by actual statistics of the number of Japanese entering the United States between 1907 and 1923. In the former year, there were 30,226 entries; in the latter, 5,809. During the entire period between these two years, the total number of entries was 120,317, and against this figure could be set departures totaling 111,626. The excess of entries over departures was thus only 8,681, or an annual average of 578. Other than on the West Coast, it was hard to construe this thin trickle of immigrants as the all-engulfing wave so luridly depicted by California's hysterical orators.

Nor did the total number of Japanese in this country substantiate the horrid fears of the Californians that a higher birth-rate among these aliens constituted a grave menace. Between 1910 and 1920 there had been an increase in the Japanese population of the entire country, as reported in the census returns for those years, from 72,157 to 111,010. This was a gain of 28,853, but neither this figure nor the 111,010 total bulked very large in a population of 105,711,000. There were actually more than twice as many Indians in the country as Japanese.

Admittedly the difficulty in the situation lay in the fact that the great majority of Japanese—71,952—were concentrated in California, and in that state they constituted some 2 per cent of the population.

Application of the general quota system contemplated in the Immigration Act, however, would have limited

the annual number of Japanese entries to the inconsequential figure of 180, or if this were not practical, a
new treaty could have been negotiated with Japan fully
meeting legitimate demands for protection from an
influx of unassimilable aliens. But California would
accept no quota. Vague fears and alarms arising from
the ability of the Japanese in certain districts to under-
bid American labor, and to farm more successfully than
native Americans because of a lower standard of living,
rendered any rational approach to the problem impossible. The West demanded exclusion, and it had won
sufficient national support for its stand to exercise a
dominating influence over Congress.

The reaction of Japan was one of angry protest from
the moment the exclusion clause was first proposed. It
constituted the discrimination against which the Japanese delegation at Versailles had attempted to provide
in its demand for a racial equality clause in the Covenant of the League of Nations. Public opinion could
not interpret the movement to bar Japanese other than
as a national insult.

In full recognition of the justification for this feeling
in Japan, Secretary Hughes made every effort to dissuade Congress from passing the law. "I regret to be
compelled to say," he wrote the chairman of the House
Immigration Committee, "that I believe such legislative
action would largely undo the work of the Washington
Conference on Limitation of Armament, which so
greatly improved our relations with Japan."

It is possible that Administration pressure, upheld
by public opinion in the Eastern part of the United
States which did not share the West's violent anti-Jap-

anese feeling, might have secured modification of the exclusion clause. But at this point the Japanese Ambassador employed a phrase, in a further note of protest against the proposed legislation, which overnight solidified Congressional support in its favor. "I realize, as I believe you do," he wrote Secretary Hughes, "the grave consequences which the enactment of the measure retaining that particular provision would inevitably bring upon the otherwise happy and mutually advantageous relations between the two countries."

Into the charged atmosphere of Congressional debate on the perils of the Japanese invasion, the phrase "grave consequences" fell like a thunderbolt. It was torn from its context by the proponents of exclusion and brandished as the final, compelling argument to prove the necessity of immediate action to restrain Japan. Not only did Congressmen from the West interpret this statement—which only echoed what Secretary Hughes had already said—as unwarranted interference in our domestic politics and an attempt on the part of a foreign envoy to dictate to Congress. Representatives and Senators from all over the country gave to "grave consequences" its most sinister connotation. "I, for one," stated Senator Reed, expressing the well-nigh universal reaction in Congress, "feel compelled on account of that veiled threat, to vote in favor of exclusion."

There was no further question in regard to passage of the bill. A phrase had carried the day. Within twenty-four hours the House had accepted the exclusion clause; three days later the Senate fell in line. Japanese immigrants were to be completely barred from the United States regardless of the affront to Japan such a law represented. "Persistent agitation, inadvertently abetted by diplomatic ineptitude and culminating in Senatorial hysteria," in the words of a bulletin of the Foreign Policy Association, "threatened needlessly to wreck the most important achievement of the Washington Conference." Passage of the Act, indeed, could be characterized in even stronger terms as a gratuitous insult to a friendly people which constituted as stupid a move as may well be found in all the annals of Congress.

The immediate reaction in Japan went far toward justifying both Secretary Hughes's and the Japanese Ambassador's fears that "grave consequences" would result from the passage of the bill—unless the Congressional interpretation is accepted that grave consequences necessarily meant a threat of war. For Japanese public opinion was so shocked and embittered that a fierce wave of anti-American feeling swept over the country. Abuse was heaped upon America for betraying her trust and imperiling peace. "We do not like war," the *Nichi Nichi* declared solemnly, "but the sense of honor dictates us to take up the gauntlet thrown down at us."

Meetings of protest were held at which the United States was denounced in the most violent terms; a resolution attacking the exclusion bill passed the Diet; a movement was started to boycott American goods; and the demand was widely voiced that all missionaries in Japan should be deported. In a patriotic demonstration against this attack upon Japan's honor, a number of Japanese youths dramatically committed hara-kiri.

Fortunately public opinion on this side of the Pacific met the wave of anti-American agitation with relative calm. There were jingoistic outbursts in California;

BARON TANAKA

once again rumors of impending war inspired head-
lines in the sensational press. One Congressman proposed an immediate conference of the white nations
to meet the Japanese menace. But more widespread was
a somewhat guilty popular feeling that Japan had very
good cause for being incensed. In the East the form
in which the Immigration Act had been passed was generally regretted, and the essential justice of Japan's position admitted. It was felt that we had done the cause of
peace in the Pacific a grave disservice.

The official attitude of both countries also served
greatly to allay popular excitement. The Japanese Government renewed in vigorous terms its protest against
exclusion; the United States Government defended the
course Congress had chosen to follow. But no further
reference to grave consequences crept into the Japanese
notes, and Secretary Hughes was as conciliatory in his
replies as circumstances permitted. The Japanese Foreign Minister stated that discrimination was "contrary
to the dictates of justice and fairness," but he carefully
explained to the Diet that there had been no suggestion of inferiority in our exclusion of Japanese immigrants, and he took pains to point out that the law
had been opposed by the President and the State Department.

It is almost equally easy to exaggerate or to minimize
the importance of the immigration controversy. There
was at no time any real likelihood of its being magnified
into a cause for war; it did not in any sense constitute
as serious a clash as the basic American-Japanese controversy over the status of China. No Japanese Government would have allowed a question involving the im-

migration of a handful of its subjects seriously to jeopardize international relations in view of the known attitude of our Government. Nevertheless, in its effect upon the Japanese people, the Exclusion Act was of very grave import and had far-reaching repercussions.

It played directly into the hands of the militaristic elements in Japan and strengthened immeasurably the popular appeal of all those who advocated an aggressive, imperialistic foreign policy. The nationalists were given an unlooked-for opportunity to attack the sincerity of the conciliatory and peaceful attitude toward Japan which America officially professed. They had a strong case when they declared that Japan could not expect from the West any real support in working out her problems and should consequently rely wholly upon the force of her own arms to defend national interests.

"An explosive force has been lodged in the Japanese mind," wrote one Japanese writer, "an explosive force that those who seek ways of international peace and progressive democracy in Japan will have to reckon with for decades to come. . . . The grave consequences flow from the fact that it is now very difficult for any Japanese liberal to convince the conservatives and the nationalists that the process by which the immigration bill was passed was not intended to serve notice on Japan that she need expect no more coöperation from America."

The ultimate results of the Exclusion Act were to strengthen the countermovement of Asia for the Asiatics. Its fruits were to ripen in 1931.

In the years immediately following this incident in the history of American-Japanese relations, the Far East attracted even greater public interest consequent upon developments which concerned not only America and Japan but the entire world. For that amorphous institution known as the Chinese Republic went through a new crisis. The revolutionary process estopped in 1911 by the militarists' seizure of power had been renewed. The Nationalists, imbued with the idealistic doctrines of Sun Yat-sen, dramatically marched north. Through force of arms and through force of propaganda, they broke down all resistance and won a series of victories which enabled them to overthrow the reactionary régime at Peking and establish a government at Nanking which could claim, with at least greater warrant than any of its predecessors, to speak for a united China.

The rise of Nationalism in China derived a great part of its strength from two important sources: Communistic propaganda and intense antiforeign agitation. So strong was the Communist movement that its victory was averted only by a narrow margin. The antiforeign feeling continued to make headway. Hatred of the foreign interloper, who still kept China in the straight-jacket of tariff control and extraterritoriality despite the pledges of the Washington Conference, who still maintained foreign concessions and legation guards at Peking, surged through the Chinese masses. It was fanned to a fever heat by propaganda against imperialism, skilfully utilized by the Nationalists to cement together their own followers.

Confronted with this dangerous phenomenon, the Powers followed an uncertain and vacillating policy which appeared to inflame the antiforeign feeling still further. A series of tragic "incidents" provided the Nationalist agitators with graphic evidence to prove the ruthlessness of imperialism, while every concession to their demands served to convince the Chinese that only through force could they hope to win international equality. The problem of China became as momentous a one as it had been at the close of the nineteenth century, leading to a somewhat analogous situation. The coöperative policy involving joint military action for the protection of foreign interests, which the powers for a time followed, bore a certain resemblance to intervention in 1900. But the Nationalists, unlike the Boxers, had more strings to their bow than antiforeignism. They had a program; they had leadership; and they had the determination to establish a government which could assert China's independence of foreign domination.

The Powers were gradually compelled to realize that here was a force which they could not resist short of waging war. They had to recognize the Nationalist Government, and in so doing, they had also to recognize China's inherent right to international equality. In a new series of treaties governing the Republic's relations with the outside world, the principle of tariff autonomy and China's right to abolition of extraterritoriality were conceded. While the Nationalists had by no means made China safe for democracy, and there was no real assurance of the stability of the Nanking régime, the West could follow no other course.

The policy of Japan during this period, when internal strife in China appeared to open the way to further aggression, was at first highly exemplary. Addressing the Diet early in 1926, Foreign Minister Shidehara explicitly declared that the maintenance of internal peace, even in Manchuria, was China's responsibility, and its assumption by Japan would be inconsistent with the basic principles of the Washington treaties. "By taking such a course," he said, "we would forfeit our national honor and pride once for all. In no case and by no means, can we be a party to so important an action."

So conciliatory a policy naturally aroused the Japanese militarists, and largely through their influence in the Privy Council a change of government was effected which for a time brought into power a more aggressive ministry. Thus early in 1927 Premier Tanaka adopted a "positive policy" which sought to protect more actively Japan's interests in China and especially to maintain her special position in Manchuria. The intervention of Japanese troops in Shantung and their occupation of Tsinan for a time blocked the Chinese Nationalists' advance on Peking, and in Manchuria definite measures were taken by the Japanese high command to prevent the spread of revolutionary disturbances to those provinces.

This active interference in Chinese affairs might have been expected to arouse some forebodings in the United States, but the unsettled conditions in the Far East created a certain amount of sympathy for Japan's strong stand. There was no very great divergence between her policy and that of this country during the period when the final results of China's antiforeign outbreak could not be foreseen. America was too anxious to protect her own nationals and property to cavil at whatever measures Japan might take. American troops were also involved in operations on Chinese soil.

Furthermore, there was no evidence that even this new "positive policy" contemplated any further extension of Japanese political power in China. Baron Tanaka made it clear that Japan felt protection of her interests in Manchuria involved her national existence, but he firmly reiterated that "we have no aggressive or territorial designs in that or any other part of China." In view of what the other Powers were doing or had done at various stages of the revolutionary movement, there were slight grounds for objecting to Japan's defense of her rights.

While her attitude was interpreted in China as foreshadowing more drastic developments, public opinion in this country consequently never became greatly excited over the "positive policy." The old charge of imperialism was conspicuously absent in such comments upon Japan as appeared in the press. No threat was apparent to the Washington treaties or to the Open Door. Japan was indeed largely ignored in the confused popular discussions of what was going to happen in China, and it was safely assumed that there had been no real change in the liberalism which had replaced the aggressive program symbolized by the Twenty-One Demands.

Such confidence soon appeared fully justified when domestic attacks upon the Tanaka ministry led to a new swing of the political pendulum bringing a liberal government back into power. Baron Shidehara returned to the Foreign Office in 1929, and such fears as the skeptics had entertained that Japan would take advantage of civil war in China were largely dissipated.

The storm of controversy over immigration having been successfully weathered and the more critical period of Chinese revolution having been survived without any attack upon the status quo in the Pacific, it remained for the London Naval Treaty, concluded in 1930, to set a further seal upon this era of good-will in American-Japanese relations. Japan had signed the Kellogg anti-war treaty, although with the understanding that Manchuria fell within the field covered by self-defense; she now signed this new naval accord. No greater vindication of the essential soundness of the spirit of international coöperation ushered in by the Washington Conference could have been asked.

It has only recently been revealed by how narrow a margin the Japanese liberals secured ratification of the London Treaty. If their victory furnished proof that they were still in the ascendancy, the bitter fight against the agreement indicated even more graphically that the militarists were determined to win back the power they saw slipping from them. Those Japanese who believed that their country could not afford to accept the limitations which the West was placing upon their territorial and military expansion were strengthened in their resolve to act next time under circumstances in which they could command full popular support.

The Japanese delegation had gone to the London Conference with instructions to insist upon a minimum strength for large cruisers and other auxiliary vessels according to a 10-10-7 ratio, as opposed to the 5-5-3 ratio for battle-ships accepted at Washington, and also to demand equality in submarines on the basis of existing strength. This position was in direct conflict with the American demand for application of the 5-5-3 ratio to these smaller vessels. After prolonged negotiations a compromise was reached by the American and Japanese delegates. It provided for a Japanese ratio of approximately 70 per cent the total strength of all auxiliary vessels, but a lower ratio of 60 per cent for large cruisers. While parity in submarines was agreed upon, an upper limit of 52,700 tons was set instead of the 78,000 tons sought by Japan.

Against the advice of its naval experts and in the face of the outspoken opposition of the Admiralty to the lower ratio for large cruisers, the Japanese Government decided to accept this compromise. It had become convinced that it was absolutely essential to do so if any treaty was to be concluded at all, and the Hamaguchi Ministry deliberately challenged military and naval domination of the civil government in order to make this gesture of international friendship. "The successful negotiation of the Three-Power agreement," the London *Times* declared, "owed much to the statesmanship and sense of reality of the Japanese Government," but it could hardly know to how great a test this statesmanship was to be put in winning ratification for the treaty.

The issue as it developed in Japan was whether the Supreme War Council, strongly opposing the treaty as infringing upon Japan's need for self-defense, or the Government, which declared national interests were

BARON SHIDEHARA

adequately safeguarded, should exercise the right to direct foreign policy. Premier Hamaguchi valiantly upheld his position, refused to concede the right of the Supreme War Council to determine such a question, and eventually forced the Privy Council to recommend ratification of the treaty by unequivocally demanding that it uphold his contentions.

It was an unprecedented victory for the principle of responsible Cabinet Government and the most drastic defeat the Supreme War Council had ever suffered. It had been won only through the support of Prince Saionji, the Genro, and Count Makino, Lord Privy Seal. Nevertheless, the Government's stand had received widespread popular support. Both at home and abroad this triumph of liberalism was enthusiastically hailed as proving that Japan had completely thrown over the military clique which had dragged her into her Asiatic adventures. She was believed to be more firmly committed than ever to the principle of collective security in the Pacific.

America appeared to have no further reason to fear Japanese imperialism. Once again Franklin Delano Roosevelt minimized the dangers of any disturbance in the Pacific, stating that there was "no real need for much more than a police force on the seas of the civilized world today." In a friendly address in Tokyo, our Ambassador compared the purpose of Japan to maintain peace in the Orient to our like purpose to maintain it in the Western Hemisphere. "Japan," he said, "must and will be the guardian of peace in the Pacific."

Whatever causes for conflict or controversy might once have existed, they appeared to be thoroughly liquidated as 1930 gave way to 1931. The London Conference crowned the success of the Washington Conference. There was no problem involving the Orient which could not under these happy circumstances admit of peaceful solution.

So it was with something of a shock that, on September 19, 1931, a slightly incredulous public read in its morning papers that Japanese troops had occupied Mukden and that the military occupation of Manchuria was under way.

CHAPTER XIII

JAPANESE IMPERIALISM

A WORLD DEEPLY INVOLVED IN THE THROES OF DEPRES-
sion—Great Britain went off the gold standard
three days after the attack on Mukden—was completely
taken by surprise by this renewal of Japan's offensive
against China and its threat to the stability of the Pacific. The Japanese Foreign Office itself had no immediate warning of a step taken by the military on their
own initiative and involving a complete shift in national policy. Nevertheless, behind the peaceful façade
of Baron Shidehara's conciliatory attitude, events had
been slowly moving toward some such outbreak.

For while Japan had been compelled in 1922 to
forego whatever ambitions she may have harbored to
consolidate her wartime gains in Shantung and Siberia,
the determination to maintain her position in Manchuria had never been relinquished. All elements
within the Empire agreed upon the necessity of unquestioned domination of this adjacent territory. It was
a first line of national defense and a source of raw
materials vital to Japan's economic status. And largely
ignored by the outside world, the program of the Chinese Nationalists was definitely undermining the Japanese position in Manchuria. Noting these developments in the summer of 1931, a prophetic Russian
observer unqualifiedly stated that the situation clearly

meant "that at any moment one can expect some decisive action on the part of Japanese imperialism."

Had the more liberal forces standing for faithful adherence to the principle of coöperation in the Pacific
been able to demonstrate that Japanese political and
economic security was fully guaranteed under the new
dispensation, they might possibly have averted an open
clash with China. But they could not do so. The West
had made no concessions to the needs of a rising nation
for greater freedom of activity in the outside world.
Japan felt unfairly restricted. Her rapidly increasing
population demanded an outlet, and America slammed
the door in the face of a handful of immigrants. Industry sought new sources of raw material and new
markets, and here were the Chinese Nationalists attempting to bar her from the most logical field of
development in near-by Manchuria.

Moreover, the country's military leaders were driven
toward a drastic assertion of Japan's rights in China for
two compelling reasons: the belief that it was Japan's
destiny to dominate the Orient and to expand overseas;
and the realization that only through a dramatic move
toward the attainment of these ambitions could they
uphold their own position in Japan's national life.
Smarting under the defeat to their policy in the accords
signed at Washington and in the London Naval Treaty,
they felt that their only hope lay in action. And in the
vague belief that somehow an aggressive policy toward
China would bring a solution to economic ills for which
international coöperation seemed to offer no remedy,
the people of Japan were ready to support them.

Under such circumstances the efforts of the Nationalist authorities in Manchuria to weaken Japan's position and a series of disputes, which appeared impossible of solution due to the basic conflict in interest between the two countries, set the stage for decisive events.

The basic forces behind Japan's underlying urge toward expansion, as it reached its climax in 1931, were at once political and economic. Her vulnerable position as a small island Empire, in many ways analogous to the position of Great Britain, had steadily driven her along this course as a safeguard for national security. The need for protection from more powerful neighbors had first led to intervention in Korea and Manchuria on the theory that a defensive frontier had to be established on the mainland. Japan could not allow any rival Power to become so strongly established in these near-by territories as to be able to dominate her.

The resolve of Japanese statesmen that their country should play a major rôle in world politics, an ambition natural enough in view of the patriotic, aggressive character of the Japanese people, strengthened this desire to win overseas dominion. Japan, as had so many nations before her, sought an Empire which would satisfy national aspirations for a place in the sun if for no other reason than that she felt entitled to a place in the sun. Too late to compete on equal terms with the Western nations in their imperialistic expansion, she was all the more determined to establish her supremacy in the Far East. The expulsion of Russia from Manchuria was thus not enough. Japan was vitally concerned in holding these Chinese provinces as the corner-stone of her own continental empire.

As part of her effort to achieve real national independence, geographical circumstance had also dictated for Japan a program of intensive industrialization. Limited in space and resources, the importation of raw goods and their conversion into manufactured products for foreign export, represented the only means whereby the economic progress essential to political power could be maintained. The sinews of war had to be provided in an imperialistic world if Japan's emergence from her centuries of isolation was not to lead to her submergence as a national entity.

This economic program thus provided a further reason for Japan to look to the Asiatic mainland. It was the potential source of many of the materials she lacked; it was the most accessible market for the goods she had to export. In a peaceful world these materials might possibly be obtained elsewhere more advantageously, and exports would normally flow to the most natural market. But Japan could hardly be expected to predicate her national development on the premise of a peaceful world. Observing the course of Western imperialism, it was inevitable that she should act upon the theory that controlled raw materials and controlled markets were essential to her. Through the availability of its resources, Manchuria thus became not only a first line of military defense and the corner-stone of Empire, but an economic life-line.

These resources, despite marked limitations, served to supplement very materially Japan's own inadequacies. In 1930, Manchuria accounted for approximately 44 per cent of the imports in her important trade with China. She relied heavily upon Manchurian soy beans and bean cake, imported large quantities of millet and wheat, while one-third of her pig-iron imports and three-fourths of her coal imports came largely from this territory.

Still more important were the Japanese investments in Manchuria. They had expanded steadily since acquisition of the South Manchuria Railway and amounted to approximately 63 per cent of the total invested in China, which was in turn 82 per cent of all Japan's foreign investments. Totaling 1,100,400,000 yen, of which the largely government-owned railway accounted for 637,800,000 yen, some 35 per cent of these investments were in transport, 15 per cent in mines, and 13 per cent in real estate.

Manchuria as a source of raw materials, rather than as a market for Japanese goods, gave the territory its primary importance. If food supplies came first, its iron ore and coal were felt to be almost equally essential. Neither are of very high grade—in some quarters Manchuria's resources have been greatly overestimated —but total coal reserves have been placed at 2,700,-000,000 metric tons and all grades of iron ore at 740,000,000 tons. In addition, Manchuria has important deposits of gold, lead, tungsten and silver, oil shale for possible distillation, and is a potential source for both cotton and wool.

The industrial development of Japan since the middle of the nineteenth century has had a further effect which is sometimes advanced as a more compelling reason for Japanese expansion than either military or strictly economic considerations. This is the rapid increase in the country's population which has created the general impression, zealously fostered by Japanese publicists, that pressure from this source has inexorably forced her to seek new outlets for her people. Psychologically overpopulation is an important factor in the situation; actually it has only indirect bearing upon Japanese expansion.

The population problem in Japan has those ironic aspects often associated with population growth in European countries. The industrialization program undertaken to enable the country to play its full rôle in world affairs is largely responsible for the increase in population, and this increase is now forcing more and more intensive industrialization to support the mounting number who cannot comfortably subsist on domestic food supplies. In adopting the ways of the West, Japan has created a Frankenstein monster.

The gain in Japan's population is thus not a peculiar phenomenon arising from any special fecundity on the part of the Japanese people. The rate of increase generally parallels that previously experienced by other countries which went through their industrial revolutions at an earlier date.

The population in 1872, the first census after Commodore Perry's visit in the middle of the century, was 33,000,000, and in so far as available records make such a deduction possible, it had been at approximately this level throughout the previous century and a quarter. Thereafter it began to increase rapidly. In the next sixty years it almost doubled, totaling approximately 65,000,000 in 1931.

But between 1801 and 1851, a fifty-year period, the population of Great Britain had doubled under somewhat comparable circumstances, and in the next half century it showed a further gain of 82 per cent. The highest birth-rate recorded for Japan in any one year is 36 per thousand; England in 1880 had a rate of 34 per thousand. British population is now almost stable; in Japan there is still a natural increase of almost 1,000,000 a year, more than in any other country except Russia.

But while Japan cannot escape for some time from the pressure of an increasing number of people for whom work and subsistence must somehow be provided, there is no reason to believe that such pressure will continue indefinitely. As in other parts of the world, the current trend is toward population stability if not an eventual decline. Japan's birth-rate is already falling, and she should attain her maximum population within another generation. Some estimates state that it will be reached in 1950 with a total of 80,000,000.

At no time, moreover, has emigration offered a solution for Japan's population problem. There is no validity whatsoever in the theory that Manchuria is important as an outlet for her surplus man-power. The number of Japanese who might move to the mainland has never constituted an important factor in the situation. Population is a vital element in Japan's expansion only in so far as the industrialization program necessary to support her people—through exchanging factory products for foodstuffs—inspires a program of imperialistic control of raw materials and foreign markets.

These political and economic motives for maintaining control of Manchuria, resulting from Japan's geographic position and lack of the resources necessary for her industrial expansion, are still further enforced by certain psychological factors. That she must dominate Manchuria is an emotional as well as a rational concept. Two wars have been fought over Manchuria; the youth of Japan are continually being impressed with the incalculable sacrifices these wars entailed.

"Patriotic sentiment, the paramount need for military defense, and exceptional treaty rights all combine to create the claim to a 'special position' in Manchuria," the Lytton Report stated. "The Japanese conception of this 'special position' is not limited to what is legally defined in treaties and agreements whether with China or with other States. Feelings and historical associations, which are the heritage of the Russo-Japanese War, and pride in the achievements of Japanese enterprise in Manchuria for the last quarter century, are an indefinable but real part of the Japanese claim to a 'special position.' It is natural, therefore, that the Japanese use of this expression in diplomatic language should be obscure, and that other States should have found it difficult, if not impossible, to recognize it by international instruments."

Even those liberals who were prepared to accept the rebuff to Japanese ambitions implicit in the Washington accords continued to recognize the force of these associations. They differed from the militarists in their attitude toward Manchuria only in the methods to be pursued. They were ready to follow a more conciliatory policy in which commercial penetration rather than direct political action would achieve the desired objective of paramount Japanese influence. Their program, however, was not meeting with sufficient success either to answer the demand of the militarists for a more aggressive policy, or to assuage the growing unrest created by depressed economic conditions which, rightly or wrongly, were popularly attributed to weak and ineffective governmental policies at home and abroad.

While the more enlightened industrial and trading interests of the country may have realized that a vigorous policy on the continent offered an inadequate solution of Japan's difficulties, not so the agricultural and colonial interests for which the army has always been the spokesman.

"Being embedded so deeply in the life and traditions of the land," a Japanese historian, Tatsuji Takeuchi, has written, "we can easily see that, to these famine-stricken farmers and nationalistic youths, Manchuria seemed to offer an immediate and inviting solution of their problem. The psychology of the time can be appreciated better when we remember that the majority of the men in the army and navy have always come from country districts, that they sacrificed most in the two wars fought on the plains of Manchuria, and consequently that, upon the least suggestion or provocation, they could be made to support any policy which might strengthen their ties with this fair land."

These were the material and intangible factors behind Japan's attitude toward Manchuria in 1931, and in the light of current developments in China, determined measures to defend her interests became almost inevitable. For there was no question that the activities of the Chinese Nationalists threatened even those rights and privileges which were supposedly secured by international treaties. Widespread anti-Japanese boycotts, fostered and encouraged by the Nationalists, had already had a seriously adverse effect upon Japan's trade. Even more harmful measures were being promoted, particularly the encouragement of Chinese railway construction, which would serve to drain away the business of the South Manchuria Railway.

Japan had made a first attempt to protect herself from encroachments on what she considered definitely Japanese preserves by barring the Chinese Nationalists' advance into Manchuria during the period of civil warfare. In 1928, however, Governor Chang Hsueh-liang had gone over to their camp. Japan was then powerless to prevent the steady infiltration of Nationalist influence and had no effective means of checking a policy of persistent disregard of treaty rights, or of circumventing a railway building program which had the obvious aim of nullifying her commercial privileges.

In subsequent justification of the decisive move which materialized on September 18th, the Tokyo Government charged the Nanking Government with scores of infractions of recognized Japanese privileges. The defense made by China largely constituted a denial of the validity of the treaty rights on which Japan based her case. But the legalistic merits of the two nations' contentions are of only the slightest academic interest. Nor is it at all profitable to weigh their relative moral rights.

Regardless of the immediate provocation for Japan's attack, involving a still obscure bomb explosion on the tracks of the South Manchuria Railway, the essential factors in 1931 were two: the Chinese Nationalists in

Manchuria had set foot on a definite movement to undermine Japan's position, and an opposing program was rapidly maturing in Japan to reassert and strengthen that position.

CHAPTER XIV

MANCHURIA, 1931

AS THE JAPANESE TROOPS PROCEEDED, EFFICIENTLY and methodically, to the occupation of Mukden, Antung, and other Manchurian cities in the last week of September, 1931, disarming the Chinese troops and seizing all public buildings, there was every evidence that the army was acting according to a carefully pre-arranged plan. The development of a real crisis in the politics of the Far East could not be ignored.

China promptly protested to the League of Nations and apprised the signatories of the Kellogg Pact of what she termed an unprovoked act of aggression. The League immediately urged the two nations to withdraw their troops, for the protection of both nationals and property, and undertook consultations with the Chinese and Japanese representatives at Geneva to the end of securing a peaceful settlement of the dispute. The United States, on September 23rd, addressed notes to both countries expressing the hope that they would "cause their respective military forces to refrain from further hostilities."

With these developments the curtain on this Far Eastern drama was officially raised, and for a time the prompt intervention of the outside world appeared to hold out some prospect that an accord might be reached. Japan's delegates at Geneva gave every assurance of their country's desire for peace. They declared that the troops would be withdrawn as speedily as possible and emphatically disclaimed any Japanese design upon Chinese territory. Even when these assurances were almost daily belied by cables from the Far East telling of further hostile measures, the belief persisted that it was only the Kwantung army which was out of hand, and that the Japanese Government would soon assert its authority and enforce a more peaceful policy.

The attitude of both the League and the United States was predicated upon this assumption in the early days of the controversy. They carefully refrained from taking any specific action which might serve to make the task of the civilians in the Japanese Government more difficult. But their forbearance was completely ineffectual. The military spirit in Japan was too strong, it exercised too powerful a hold upon the popular imagination, for the more liberal elements in the country to effect a change of policy once troops had begun to move in Manchuria. While the diplomats suavely talked of peace, the Government itself was being confronted with a series of *faits accomplis* which completely nullified its efforts to localize the conflict and placate foreign opinion.

There was no longer any question of dual diplomacy in Japan. The War Department had completely supplanted the Foreign Office in the direction of national policy. The rebuffs administered in the ratification of the naval treaties, and through the conciliatory policy of Baron Shidehara, were to be revenged by the exercise of complete control over the course of events in Manchuria. The army insisted upon full settlement of all outstanding questions with China, and on military occupation until complete satisfaction was obtained. As its leaders became more certain of public support, they further made it clear that their conception of the security to which Japan was entitled in Manchuria necessitated full control over the entire territory.

The pious hopes of the statesmen in Geneva and Washington that a little mild pressure would restrain Japan could not be maintained in the face of these developments. The rapid extension of military operations furnished indisputable proof that Japan's real objective had become the fulfilment of the thwarted ambitions of a decade earlier. With the army prepared to resist any attempt upon the part of the League, or any outside agency, to intervene in the situation, there was little likelihood that there would this time be any voluntary retreat.

As the crisis became more acute, the League sought the coöperation of the United States, as a signatory of the Kellogg Pact, in its efforts to hold Japan back. It did not seek in vain. Secretary Stimson assured it that, acting independently, the American Government would endeavor to reinforce whatever the League did and would not hesitate to make clear its interest in the situation. "It is most desirable," the American Secretary of State said, "that the League in no way relax its vigilance and in no way fail to assert all the pressure and authority within its competence toward regulating the action of China and Japan in the premises."

When a little later the Council, over Japan's vehement objections, invited the United States to send a representative to its meeting, Secretary Stimson accepted. For a brief time the astounding spectacle was presented of an emissary of a Republican Administration, which had always held the Wilsonian League of Nations anathema, actually sitting at the council table in Geneva, authorized "to participate in the discussions of the Council when they relate to the possible application of the Kellogg-Briand Pact."

There was never a time in the League's history when its opportunity to assert its authority was greater. Public opinion throughout the world was strongly convinced that Japan had violated her treaty obligations and was using force as an instrument of national policy. It could have been counted upon to support any firm course of action the League adopted. But in these first sessions on the Manchurian dispute in the fall of 1931, the League lost a chance which never again recurred under the same circumstances. It hesitated and wavered; it made no immediate effort to apply either economic or military sanctions; and it thereby served notice upon Japan that it did not have the strength of its convictions or the courage to enforce them.

More than that, the vacillating policy followed at Geneva clearly demonstrated to all the world that as an instrument to enforce the sanctity of international obligations, the League acted upon expediency rather than upon principle. Dominated by Great Britain and France, nations whose interests in the Far East were better served by friendship with Japan than by arousing her hostility, it made caution its rule. Although America for once was willing to coöperate, the possible risks of applying sanctions against Japan were held too dangerous to justify them.

As observers of the international scene, both Germany and Italy were thus presented with an example of the League's attitude in an international crisis which unquestionably effected the formulation of their own policies. It was the League's fundamental inaction in the Manchurian dispute, rather than its belated and unsuccessful action in the Ethiopian crisis, which demonstrated its ineffectiveness as an instrument for the maintenance of world peace whenever a determined nation chose to ignore it.

Just as the failure of the League to take a decisive stand against Japanese expansion proved that Great Britain and France did not feel the issue sufficiently important to face the hazards of active intervention, American willingness to coöperate with the League at this time indicated a conviction on our part that our interests were materially threatened. We assumed the position that we were solely interested in fulfilling our obligations as a joint guarantor of international peace, but actually we were no more acting upon principle in urging a strong opposition to Japan than were Great Britain and France in minimizing the need for such a policy. For the point need hardly be stressed that a threat to peace in any other part of the world, however definitely it meant a violation of the anti-war treaty, would not have led to American coöperation with the League. Our strict aloofness in the war between Italy and Ethiopia four years later stands as indisputable proof of this. We took the stand we did in 1931 because the Administration felt it necessary, from the standpoint of national interest, to do what it could to safeguard our power and prestige in the Far East in the face of the attacks of Japanese imperialism.

Public opinion on the whole supported Secretary Stimson in his policy of coöperation with the League. Japan's advance had created a sensation. "Territorial rape planned and executed at a moment when China is helpless and the great nations of the world enmeshed in economic difficulties," was the vivid characterization of one editorial writer. Almost any move which might restrain Japan, short of actual war, was at this juncture certain of popular support. If there was any chance of concerted international action serving to maintain peace, it was felt that America could not stand aside.

Our position inevitably aroused the strongest resentment in Japan. It was interpreted not as coöperation with the League, but as an attempt to force the League to more decisive measures than it might otherwise have taken. Once again, as at the Versailles Conference and as at the Washington Conference, America was pictured as assuming an aggressive leadership in trying to checkmate Japanese ambitions. Popular feeling in Japan swung further toward support of the militarists in their resolve to establish once and for all Japanese hegemony in Northern China.

In the meantime, further developments were taking place on both the military and the diplomatic front. By December the army had achieved all its immediate objectives and was in dominant control of the greater part of Southern Manchuria. It had forced the removal from office of all anti-Japanese factions in the Manchurian Government. Nevertheless, the Tokyo Foreign Office was at the same time expressing a desire to work with the League in seeking an equitable solution of the dispute. It was prepared to accede to proposals for the dispatch to the Far East of a commission of inquiry to ascertain the facts upon which a possible settlement might be based.

The League had no recourse other than to accept these conciliatory gestures at their face value. On December 10th, it unanimously passed a resolution, in which Japan concurred, and to which the United States subsequently gave its approval, providing for an international commission "to study on the spot and to report to the Council on any circumstance which, affecting international relations, threatens to disturb peace between China and Japan, or the good understanding between them, upon which peace depends." This resolution also took note that the two parties to the dispute had undertaken to adopt all measures necessary "to avoid any further aggravation of the situation and to refrain from any initiative which may lead to further fighting and loss of life."

The unreality of this move on the part of Geneva in the light of actual events in Manchuria was emphasized by the fact that passage of the resolution was hailed in Japan as a victory for her diplomacy, and in other countries as a triumph for the principles of the League. Its only immediate effect was to relieve the League of the necessity of any further action at this time, and momentarily to abate the criticism which was being so vigorously expressed in the League Assembly. While not everywhere in this country was the optimistic view held that Japan had in any way been compelled to modify her policy, as well informed a newspaper as the Baltimore *Sun* found in the resolution a happy augury for the future. "The League has so mobilized the forces of the world opinion and world diplomacy," it declared, "as to check Japan in her career of Manchurian aggression."

Disillusionment was not long forthcoming. An overturn in Japanese politics brought into power a government even more susceptible to military pressure than its predecessor. The appointment of General Araki as Minister of War promised a positive policy rather than a conciliatory one in future dealings with the Chinese. With army spokesmen becoming more emphatic in their demand that a vigorous program of expansion should be followed to assure peace in Asia, the Government had to swing into line. The result was a further advance into Manchurian territory and the occupation of Chinchow, in open violation of what Secretary Stimson stated were specific assurances that no such action was contemplated.

In explaining this advance, Tokyo was quoted in the American press as saying that it had become necessary as an act of self-defense. "The Japanese Government are confident," it was blandly stated, "that their prolonged forbearance and the desire strictly to adhere to stipulations of international engagements will not fail to command recognition by the public opinion of the world." But it was now too late for this. While it was widely realized that Japan had experienced grave provocation prior to the attack upon Mukden, her forbearance in subsequent months was not entirely clear.

At this point, in any event, the United States decided to supplement the inadequate action taken by the

League and to exercise independently and more directly what influence it could command. The threat to North China in the advance to Chinchow was interpreted in Washington as seriously jeopardizing American interests. It appeared to demand as drastic a protest as circumstances permitted. This took the form of identic notes to the Japanese and Chinese Governments, dispatched on January 7, 1932, which embodied that declaration of policy which has since been known as the Stimson Doctrine:

. . . In view of the present situation and of its own rights and obligations therein, the American Government deems it to be its duty to notify both the Government of the Chinese Republic and the Imperial Japanese Government that it cannot admit the legality of any situation de facto nor does it intend to recognize any treaty or agreement entered into between those governments, or agents thereof which may impair the treaty rights of the United States or its citizens in China, including those which relate to the sovereignty, the independence, or the territorial and administrative integrity of the Republic of China, or to the international policy relative to China, commonly known as the open-door policy, and that it does not intend to recognize any situation, treaty, or agreement which may be brought about by means contrary to the covenants and obligations of the pact of Paris of August 27, 1928, to which treaty both China and Japan, as well as the United States, are parties.

In making this pronouncement, Secretary Stimson felt he had every reason to expect the sympathy if not the forthright support of the British Government. It was not forthcoming. Indeed, Great Britain expressly stated that she saw no reason for addressing a similar note to Japan and professed confidence in her protestations that Chinese sovereignty would be respected. Secretary Stimson might have foreseen this reaction in view of England's attitude at Geneva and thereby avoided the disappointment he has subsequently confessed, but he went blithely ahead. America was for the time left alone as the champion of Chinese independence.

There was a varied reaction to the declaration of this policy in the United States. In some quarters it was hailed as the most important statement in regard to our foreign relations since the declaration of the Monroe Doctrine over a century earlier. Its unequivocal veto upon the recognition not only of any treaty or agreement impairing our treaty rights but of "any *situation, treaty, or agreement*" brought about contrary to provisions of anti-war pact was characterized as the most constructive step toward the maintenance of world peace which we had ever made.

On the other hand, the new doctrine was declared futile, in that our non-recognition of any situation in the Far East would not necessarily restrain Japan, and dangerous, in that it again placed us in the position of attempting to obstruct Japanese expansion by individual action. Its critics considered it but a further example of that ineffectual policy whereby the United States, in taking a stand which we were not prepared to back up, had so often succeeded in only irritating Japan.

The Stimson Doctrine actually went further than the policy proclaimed in 1915 by Secretary Bryan in regard to the Twenty-One Demands only in that it included violation of the provisions of the anti-war treaty as an added cause for non-recognition of any change in the status quo. And it was no more effective than the Bryan policy. Japan's concern was not over what this country might say, but over what we might do. In the absence of any indication that we were prepared to enforce the Stimson Doctrine by definite action, she did not allow it to alter her plans in any way.

That it had created resentment was evident in the official reply to Secretary Stimson's note. The position was assumed that unsettled conditions in China materially modified application of both the Nine Power Treaty and the Kellogg Treaty. In protecting her interests in Manchuria, Japan had acted wholly in self-defense. There was no question of violation of any treaties; there was no question of territorial aims or ambitions in Manchuria. If America was not specifically told to keep her hands off, the thinly veiled sarcasm of the concluding line of Tokyo's reply left no doubt as to how Japan felt. "It is agreeable to be assured," the note read, "that the American Government are devoting in a friendly spirit such sedulous care to the correct appreciation of the situation."

This exchange of notes did nothing to improve American-Japanese relations. Indeed, it aroused a fear that some overt act might "start the drums beating and the sabres rattling overnight." Whatever their academic opinions of the Stimson Doctrine, the possibility of its dragging us into war appalled editors throughout the country. The Washington *Evening Star* said that it "would be a monstrous injustice to the American people, a sacrifice of American lives and American treasure for which there would be no justification." In more picturesque language, the Philadelphia *Record* succinctly

GENERAL ARAKI

declared that "the American people don't give a hoot in a rain barrel who controls North China."

Secretary Stimson might well have pondered Theodore Roosevelt's advice as to the inadvisability and danger of assuming a position in Manchuria which we were not prepared to uphold by force. He had not made the slightest impression upon Japanese policy. Even if his purpose was to state certain general principles in order to win support for them by the other Powers, his assumption of the leadership in opposing Japan focused her resentment against outside interference with her policy almost entirely upon the United States. Furthermore, Stimson had assumed such an unequivocal attitude that unless it could be enforced, the United States would be left in the humiliating position of having to admit, either tacitly or actually, that it had made a meaningless and futile gesture.

The world was gradually becoming almost reconciled to the spectacle of Japan overrunning Manchuria when it was again startled, late in January, 1932, by an aggressive forward movement by Japanese naval forces in the very heart of China. This attack bore no direct relation to the occupation of Manchuria. It had even less warrant in international law. But it resulted in an outbreak of Japanese-Chinese hostilities in Shanghai which for a time held the center of the world stage and seemed to hold even more definite threats of actual war.

In an effort to break an anti-Japanese boycott which the Chinese had adopted in protest against the seizure of Manchuria, certain demands had been made upon the Chinese Mayor of Shanghai. Without awaiting the concessions he was prepared to make, the Japanese proceeded to occupy a part of the Chinese city. They were met by strong resistance and thereupon opened a bombardment.

For a time it appeared that in this adventure Japan was to be checked by the only weapon capable of restraining her—imposition of actual force. It was not offered by the again protesting Powers, although the complicated situation in Shanghai led to the summoning of troops to protect the International Settlement. A Chinese army for several weeks valiantly but futilely resisted the Japanese invaders. No war was declared. The Chinese Government preferred to fight its battles in Geneva. But until the foreign representatives in Shanghai finally succeeded in bringing about a truce, it was war in fact if not in theory.

This clash of the armed forces of the two nations had no permanent results of importance, but it served to emphasize even more dramatically than anything that had happened in Manchuria, the aggressive character of Japan's new policy toward China. While Tokyo took it upon itself gravely to rebuke the Powers for their "unfriendly and thoughtless attitude regarding a matter in which Japan finds her very national existence at stake," world opinion could find nothing to condone in this reckless application of military power in Shanghai.

Japan had "outlawed herself by her campaign of brutality," the American press declared. "Insane imperialism," "running amuck," "beyond the pale of civilized warfare," were the current characterizations of her policy. So strong did popular feeling become that an imposing group of educators and editors, headed by Newton D. Baker and A. Lawrence Lowell, petitioned President Hoover in favor of American participation in an international boycott. "Economic pressure," their petition stated, "would certainly stop the present bloodshed." An American Boycott Association was also formed, with the qualified backing of the Federal Council of Churches, to further unofficial action in banning Japanese imports.

Neither of these movements made any real headway. For all its moral indignation, the American public had no desire to become seriously embroiled with Japan. It recognized the dangers which any strict application of economic sanctions would create in view of the complete control of the military over Japanese policy. "The best way to advance the cause of war between this country and Japan," Senator Borah declared caustically, and he reflected the predominant view of the public. The Stimson Doctrine had carried us as far along the road of open opposition to Japan as most Americans wanted to go, if not somewhat farther.

It was also becoming increasingly clear that in its assumption of world leadership of the anti-Japanese forces, the United States was receiving only half-hearted support from the European Powers. The failure of Great Britain and France to provide more aggressive leadership in the early stages of the dispute had indicated that they could not be counted upon to support any such movement as the application of sanctions. Now they were demonstrating an actually sympathetic attitude toward Japan. Secure in their belief that friendship with Tokyo, whatever its policy toward China, was to their interest, they had no idea of helping pull American chestnuts out of the fire.

On theoretical grounds they would still have liked to see the League's prestige enhanced as an arbiter of international disputes, but they would not run any risk in endeavoring to make its writ good in this distant part of the world. Prepared to take as strong a moral stand as their obligations to uphold the peace treaties appeared tó render necessary, their original opposition to Japan was melting away under the realization that she could not now be restrained from winning complete control of Manchuria except by military force.

Under the circumstances there was nothing the United States could do. Sanctions were of no value unless they had the full international backing which neither Great Britain nor France was willing to extend to them. Short of intervention and war, our hands were tied.

Faithful to our traditional adherence to the principles of the Open Door, Secretary Stimson found it difficult to accept the realities of this situation. He still appeared to harbor the hope that, by sternly calling Japan to task, he could effect some modification of her policy. In a letter addressed to Senator Borah on February 23rd, he made a further statement of American policy, expanding the background of his non-recognition doctrine.

This letter made clear two points. The first was that the United States regarded the Nine Power Treaty, upholding the Open Door and the integrity of China, as still in full force and constituting the corner-stone of the international settlement reached at the Washington

Conference. Our willingness in 1921 to surrender our then commanding lead in battle-ship construction and to agree not to fortify Guam and the Philippines, the Secretary of State said, "was predicated upon, among other things, the self-denying covenants contained in the Nine Power Treaty." The possibility of abrogating the provisions of this treaty, he then declared, could not be discussed without considering at the same time the premises upon which they were dependent.

Having hinted at revision of the naval accords in the event of abrogation of the Nine Power Treaty, Stimson then made his second point. "Regardless of cause or responsibility," he wrote, "it is clear beyond peradventure that a situation has developed which cannot, under any circumstances, be reconciled with the obligations of the covenants of these two treaties, and that if the treaties had been faithfully observed such a situation could not have arisen."

He might have gone on to say that the international situation had thus reverted to just what it was before the Washington Conference with only one important difference: the United States no longer commanded the power and prestige to call Japan to account. As the realists in 1921 had pointed out, the naval accords had led to the establishment of effective Japanese naval supremacy in the Western Pacific. Moreover, the United States had not even built its navy up to treaty limits. Every practical consideration pointed to the necessity, especially in view of the attitude of Great Britain and France, of our acquiescing in a course of events over which we had no control. Whether we liked it or not was beside the point.

While Secretary Stimson could not entirely avoid the inescapable logic of this situation, he had still been unable to resist the temptation of emphasizing American opposition to the policy Japan was following. The Open Door tradition led him to take an even stronger stand than had been taken by his predecessors, and to that extent he strengthened Japan's belief that we were still the potential enemy which threatened the overseas expansion which she considered her natural right.

In the Far East events now crowded upon each other. While Japan had not allowed the protests of either the United States or of the League of Nations to cause her to deviate from her program, she was prepared to make one concession to world opinion. Manchuria would not be annexed. Too many times had she denied any territorial ambitions for even the Japanese Foreign Office to find any plausible excuse for such action. Instead, a local movement for independence was inspired whereby Manchuria could achieve autonomy under Japan's protection. Naturally this movement was officially declared to be wholly spontaneous. But this was such a hollow pretense that no serious doubt was ever entertained as to Tokyo's responsibility for the establishment of Manchukuo.

It was only made possible by the pressure of Japanese troops, the Lytton Commission later found. "A group of Japanese civil and military officials, both active and retired, who were in close touch with the new political movement in Japan . . . ," its report stated, "conceived, organized and carried through this movement, as a solution to the situation in Manchuria as it existed after the events of September 18th."

Nevertheless, the military spirit was now so strong in Japan that even the temporary hesitation of the Government in recognizing this new state aroused a storm of protest against what was regarded as its dilatory tactics in supporting the army. Opposition to the parliamentary régime, to any sign of concession to world opinion, was gaining headway in an hysterical wave of extreme nationalism. Having tasted the fruits of imperialism, the Japanese public demanded an even more aggressive policy. "Let the League of Nations say whatever it pleases," declared General Araki, Minister for War, at a public meeting, "let America offer whatever interference, let Russia attempt to disturb peace in Manchuria as hard as she will, let China decry Japan's action at the top of her voice, but Japan must adhere to her course unswervingly."

As a result of such propaganda a movement for the creation of a stronger government which would even more directly carry out army policies won increasing popular support. It eventually resulted, as such movements had before and were to do again, in encouraging the Japanese extremists to direct action. On May 15, 1932, a band of men in naval and military uniforms assassinated Premier Inukai. With rumors of a Fascist dictatorship filling the air, a new government was established in which the aggressive General Araki, retaining his post as War Minister, exercised the dominating influence. The army was more than ever in complete control of Japanese foreign policy.

There was now even less question than before that

Japan was utilizing her opportunities not only to suppress anti-Japanese agitation in Manchuria but very definitely to extend her sway over northern China. As her troops penetrated still farther into Manchuria, gradually achieving the conquest of the entire territory down to the Great Wall, her official spokesmen advanced the theory that it was both Japan's destiny and Japan's duty to maintain on her own terms the peace of the Far East. Fair warning was given that she would actively resent any further suggestion of interference.

"If the United States," declared former Ambassador Ishii, author of the abrogated Lansing-Ishii Agreement, "ever attempted to dominate the Asiatic continent and to prevent Japan from pacific and natural expansion in this part of the world, then, indeed, a grave situation would be created, for it is obvious that a nation with a population overcrowded to the breaking-point cannot be shut up indefinitely in a narrow strip of land."

Negotiations were now instituted with the Government of Manchukuo looking toward that state's formal recognition. Japan prepared to forestall any possible recommendations by the League of Nation's Commission of Inquiry. The time had long since passed for any compromise settlement of the Manchurian issue. When Japan, on September 15, 1932, formally recognized the new Manchurian régime, a spokesman of the Foreign Office bluntly stated: "So far as Japan is concerned, the question of Manchukuo is settled."

The protocol established two principles: first, the Manchukuoan Government, subsequently to be transformed into an empire with the former "boy Emperor" of China on the imperial throne, recognized in full all

Japanese rights in Manchuria; second, there was to be complete coöperation between the two Governments in maintaining Manchukuo's national security. To set the final seal upon this virtual protectorate, the protocol further stated that it was "understood that such Japanese forces as may be necessary for this purpose shall be stationed in Manchukuo."

It was evident that whatever the report of the League Commission, on which General McCoy served as the American representative, the only real issues now were how far the League would go in criticizing Japan's action, and whether Japan would remain a member of the League. Any idea of sanctions had been completely abandoned. While Geneva was dealing in theories, Japan was dealing in realities. The League had followed the lead of the United States in undertaking not to recognize any situation in the Far East brought about in contravention of existing treaties, but under the influence of Great Britain and France it had already, to all practical purposes, admitted its impotence in dealing with the Manchurian crisis.

The Lytton Report was in effect an outspoken condemnation of Japan's action. Without directly holding her guilty of an unprovoked act of aggression in violation of her obligations under the Nine Power Treaty, the Kellogg Treaty, and the League Covenant, it made clear the Commission's belief that Japan had had no right to attack China, had gone far beyond the bounds of legitimate self-defense, and had been largely responsible for the supposedly spontaneous independence movement in Manchuria. The Commission stated it to be a fact "that without a declaration of war a large area of what was indisputably Chinese territory has been forcibly seized and occupied by the armed forces of Japan, and has in consequence of this operation been separated from, and declared independent of the rest of China."

It consequently expressed the opinion that under prevailing circumstances a restoration of the status quo ante, or maintenance and recognition of the existing régime in Manchuria, would be equally unsatisfactory. "Such a solution," it declared, "does not appear to us compatible with the fundamental principles of existing international obligations, nor with the good under-standing between the two countries upon which peace in the Far East depends."

On these premises, the Commission outlined a pro-gram whereby Manchuria would be granted a large measure of autonomy under Chinese sovereignty, the preservation of internal order entrusted to an effective local gendarmerie, and Japan's rights recognized along lines which would afford her free participation in the economic development of Manchuria without the right to control it either economically or politically.

This proposed solution of the controversy might have been satisfactory to Japan had it been suggested and supported by the Powers at an earlier date. It recog-nized certain of the realities in the difficult relationship between China and Japan. Had it been advanced at the time of the Washington Conference as a corollary to the political and naval accords then concluded, the history of the Far East might have been very different. But in 1932 these proposals had been so far outrun by events that they were valueless. They no longer constituted a compromise between the objectives of Japanese imperialism and the underlying doctrine of Chinese independence as they would have a decade earlier. They were a demand upon Japan for surrender of a position she had successfully won, and which her militarists could not possibly have been prevailed upon to give up without war.

Into the dispute to which the Lytton Report led at Geneva it is hardly necessary to go. Japan stoutly maintained that she had acted throughout in self-defense and that she had violated no treaty obligations. She kept up a strong rear-guard action in defense of her policies. But again there was an air of unreality about the negotiations. It was clear that there was to be no turning aside, whatever was said at Geneva. In diplomatic but none the less explicit words, Foreign Minister Uchida stated the Japanese Government's belief "that any plan for erecting an edifice of peace in the Far East should be based upon the recognition that the constructive force of Japan is the mainstay of tranquillity in this part of the world." At Geneva, Ambassador Matsuoka declared that the issue involved the very existence of Japan and, when fully developed, Manchukuo would "form the corner-stone of peace in the Far East—that is our faith."

Japan would make no further concessions to world opinion. She had taken her stand and was prepared to maintain it. She had convinced herself that justice was on her side. In a remarkable statement before the League Assembly, Ambassador Matsuoka demanded on what grounds the world arrogated to itself the right to condemn Japan.

"Are you sure that the so-called world opinion will persist forever and never change?" he asked. "Humanity crucified Jesus of Nazareth two thousand years ago. And today? Can any of you assure me that the so-called world opinion can make no mistake? We Japanese feel that we are now put on trial. Some of the people in Europe and America may wish even to crucify Japan in the twentieth century. Gentlemen, Japan stands ready to be crucified! But we do believe, and firmly believe, that, in a very few years, world opinion will be changed and that we also shall be understood by the world as Jesus of Nazareth was."

The dispute at Geneva dragged on. The League felt compelled for the sake of its own badly shattered prestige to approve the recommendations of the Lytton Commission, however futile such a gesture might be. The self-respect of Japan, the Oriental need to maintain "face," forced her not only to reject them but to threaten to withdraw from the League should the other Powers accept them. Various attempts were made to reconcile conflicting views in a new formula of conciliation. But with Japanese popular opinion growing more and more restive at what it deemed the League's unwarranted intervention, Tokyo's stand stiffened. Rather than retreat from the position she had taken in Manchuria, Ambassador Matsuoka said, "our nation is prepared to undergo even the severest sanctions." Her military gave every indication of being prepared to wage war against the world.

When a vote was finally held—February 24, 1933— on an Assembly Report largely embodying the recommendations of the Lytton Commission and pledging each League member not to recognize Manchukuo, only Japan voted against it. The Japanese delegation thereupon dramatically left the Assembly room, and somewhat more than a month later, Tokyo gave formal notice of its decision to withdraw from the League.

In these negotiations at Geneva, the United States took no part. We had reverted to our independence of action. While we had refused to recognize Manchukuo and were prepared to join in the verdict of guilty which was brought against Japan at the bar of world opinion, the vacillating policy of the dominating members of the League had demonstrated that if America favored more active intervention in the Far East, we would have to intervene alone. For that we were not prepared.

In marked contrast to the more vigorous action he had taken at the beginning of the dispute, Secretary Stimson consequently replied to the League's communication of its final report with the expression of a few pious sentiments. Declaring that the United States and the League stood on common ground in regard to nonrecognition, he expressed the hope that its members would "find it possible in the light of world opinion to conform their policies to the need and desire of the family of nations that disputes between nations shall be settled by none but pacific means."

When, ten years earlier, Japan's policy in the Far East appeared to foreshadow the action she took in 1931, America had employed all the weapons of a moral force sustained by naval superiority to compel the retreat exemplified in the signature of the Washington Conference accords. We had taken the initiative in opposing Japan's further expansion in Asia, and the European Powers had followed our leadership. In 1931 we had attempted to do the same thing—and signally failed. Unsustained by force, our influence had no tangible effect in diverting Japan from her basic objective of establishing beyond further question her complete control over Manchuria.

Japan defied the United States, defied the League of Nations, and defied world opinion. On any pragmatic basis, she had done so successfully.

CHAPTER XV

ADVANCE AND RETREAT

AS THE HOOVER ADMINISTRATION PREPARED TO GIVE way to that of President Roosevelt in March, 1933, the victory of Japanese imperialism appeared fully consummated. The occupation of Jehol succeeded that of Manchuria. The frontiers of the new state of Manchukuo were pushed back to include the entire area lying north of the Great Wall between the sea and Inner Mongolia, and in another two months the Tangku truce, negotiated with the Chinese military authorities, was to set up a demilitarized zone south of the Great Wall. Dominant Japanese control of this vast area, and the continued expansion of Japanese influence in both Inner Mongolia and North China itself, symbolized the attainment of that goal toward which Japan had set out, only to be repulsed short of full achievement, in 1894, in 1904, and again in 1914.

To justify these conquests Japanese statesmen had developed a philosophy which employed all the pacific phraseology which is universally drawn upon to explain imperialist expansion. Japan was the arbiter of peace in Eastern Asia, and the measures she had taken to establish order in Manchuria had devolved upon her as a national duty. No other course had been open. Even the more liberal elements which had originally opposed an aggressive foreign policy fell in line. Noth-

237

ing succeeds like success. With Japan so firmly entrenched on the Asiatic mainland, the triumphs of the
militaristic program could not be denied.

In repeated speeches and public statements, Ambassador Saito endeavored to impress upon the American
public that Japan's real aim was the establishment of a
reign of law and order in Manchuria, and that improv-
ing conditions in the new state were eloquent testimony
of the soundness of Japanese policy. Writing in *Foreign
Affairs,* former Premier Wakatsuki took the same
ground, with the added proviso that Japan was destined
to grow and expand overseas and that intervention in
Manchuria had constituted a life and death struggle
for her. He found no reasons for American objections
to Japanese foreign policy except on the basis of a natural rivalry induced by Japan's growing prestige and
power. He calmly stated that the sole motive of her
operations in Manchuria was the stabilization of the
situation in the Far East.

The old idea of a Japanese Monroe Doctrine was also
brought out and carefully refurbished. It had first been
developed at the close of the Russo-Japanese War, and
every subsequent attempt upon the part of Japan to
secure foreign recognition of her special rights in China
had been predicated upon the principle that she was
entitled to exercise special influence in Eastern Asia
comparable to that exercised over Latin America by the
United States. "From our point of view," Viscount Ishii
wrote in his memoirs, "Japan possesses interests superior
to other Powers in China as a whole, especially in the
contiguous regions, much as the position of your coun-

try in the Western Hemisphere, especially in Mexico and Central American countries."

The Japanese delegation at Geneva, upon the occasion of the debate over the Lytton Report, had assumed for their country full responsibility for the maintenance of peace and order in the Far East; the Minister for Foreign Affairs had told the Diet that the Government was acting upon the theory that the constructive force of Japan was the mainstay of tranquillity in Eastern Asia.

Now this principle was further developed along more aggressive lines as a cloak for the assertion of even greater rights over China. It was interpreted so broadly as to pass far beyond any possible analogy with the American Monroe Doctrine upon which it was supposedly based. Whereas the underlying purpose behind our policy, even though there have been times when it has been violated, is the preservation of the independence of the Latin American republics, the clear goal of Japan's policy was the complete subordination of China to Japanese influence.

The most extreme statement upon the rôle Japan had assumed in the Far East was made by the official spokesman of the Japanese Foreign Office in April, 1934. "It goes without saying," he stated upon this occasion, "that Japan at all times is endeavoring to maintain and promote friendly relations with foreign nations, but at the same time we consider it only natural that to keep peace and order in Eastern Asia we must even act alone on our own responsibility, and it is our duty to do so. At the same time there is no country but China that is in a position to share with

Japan the responsibility for the maintenance of peace in Eastern Asia. . . .

"We oppose, therefore, any attempt on the part of China to avail herself of the influence of any other country in order to resist Japan. We also oppose any action taken by China herself calculated to play one Power against another."

This was Japan's position. No other Power had the right to interfere with any aspect of her program. In so far as relations with China were concerned, the medium through which any foreign country should negotiate on any important question was the Japanese Foreign Office. As the president of the reactionary Black Dragon Society phrased it, America could expect an amicable solution of pending problems with Japan only by keeping her hands off Far Eastern affairs and placing implicit confidence in Japan's efforts to maintain peace. "The world should be divided," he stated, "into three parts under the influence respectively of American, European, and Asiatic Monroe Doctrines."

And for her part, Japan was prepared to maintain her position by the naked force exemplified in the rule of her military.

Confronted with these developments which so clearly nullified the international policy relative to China symbolized by the Open Door, Franklin Delano Roosevelt adopted the realistic attitude Theodore Roosevelt had urged fifteen years earlier. If Japan was determined to win control of Manchuria, she could be blocked by no means other than force. And America was not prepared to use force. While it was made clear that the United

States still upheld the validity of international engagements and would not therefore depart from the Stimson Doctrine of non-recognition of Manchukuo, there were to be no further protests against Japanese political action in the Far East.

America had made a full retreat from the position she had assumed at the beginning of the century when her imperialistic ambitions were at their height. The day when the Senate heard our trade with China characterized as "the mightiest commercial fact in our future" was only a distant memory. If tradition refused to allow the complete discard of the Open Door proclaimed some thirty-five years earlier by John Hay, only by ignoring every reality could it be denied that Japan had effectively and securely swung it shut in Northern China.

An even more visible sign of this surrender of our former ambitions was the successful conclusion of the movement to grant the Philippine Islands their independence. They had been occupied to establish a foothold off the Asiatic Coast which would enable us to assert our power in the Pacific and safeguard our trade with the Far East. Senator Beveridge had eloquently declared that their possession would make us the Power that ruled the Pacific and the Power that ruled the world. Now at the very time when Japan was challenging the basic concept of our entire Far Eastern policy, we were prepared to let them go.

Little wonder that Japan felt she could ignore our protests against her actions in Manchuria as she had not been able to ignore them at the time of the Washington Conference. Possession of the Philippines may not greatly strengthen our strategic position in the Pacific. Nevertheless, our readiness to give them up at such a time told far more clearly how the American people felt toward Asiatic adventures than the reiteration of a loyalty to the Open Door which went no further than the empty words in which it was expressed.

Independence for the Filipinos had been a goal of American idealists ever since the islands had been taken over from Spain. It was in no noble, self-sacrificing mood, however, that we finally made good our pledges. The real inspiration for this step could be traced to sugar imports. Domestic beet-sugar growers gave the independence movement the force with which idealism had been unable to endow it. They resented the competition in the American market of duty-free cane-sugar. While war and peace were at stake in the Far East, these sugar interests, with other agricultural and labor allies equally opposed to the competition of Filipino products, maneuvered their independence bill through Congress. Ruled entirely by self-interest, they completely ignored any possible repercussions of their action on national policy in the Pacific.

Here and there a voice was raised to point out that independence for the Philippines constituted a move which might gravely jeopardize our prestige and influence in the Orient. The Hoover Administration was strongly opposed to it. Reports by the four principal members of the Cabinet agreed that the time was particularly inopportune to upset the prevailing balance of power in the Far East, and that passage of the proposed bill would intensify rather than ameliorate the problems which the United States faced in the Pacific.

The President's position was that it would place "both our people and the Philippine people not on the road to liberty and safety, which we can desire, but on the path leading to new and enlarged dangers to liberty and freedom itself."

Reflecting more directly the imperialistic spirit which had originally inspired occupation of the Philippines, Nicholas Roosevelt emphasized the extent to which independence would mean our withdrawal from the Far East. "It goes without saying," he wrote, "that to leave the Philippines means to abandon the Open Door policy in China and definitely to surrender American hopes of winning a dominant commercial position in the Far East."

Nevertheless, the movement went steadily forward in an atmosphere which the New York *Times* characterized as demonstrating "a sordidness of spirit which an impartial world will condemn, and of which we ourselves ought to be ashamed." There was little liberalism and less imperialism in the Senatorial debates. When Vandenberg spoke of the dangers in which the United States might become embroiled by the retention of responsibility without authority during the transitional period before the Philippine Commonwealth would attain complete sovereignty, he talked largely to an empty chamber. Sugar and cocoanut oil were the bases for debate, and the bill passed largely because of the prevailing belief, as expressed by Senator Capper, that "the Senate owes a first and complete duty to the farmers of the United States."

President Hoover vetoed it, but no attention was paid to his message outlining the risks involved. The House overruled his action within two hours, and four days later the Senate followed its lead. On January 17, 1933 —the League was debating its final report in regard to Manchukuo and Japan was preparing to advance into Jehol—the Philippine Islands were offered independence.

Application of a program so completely at variance with that followed at the opening of the century was somewhat delayed. The Philippine legislature refused to accept the offer of independence in the particular form in which it was offered them, and not until President Roosevelt came into office did Congress agree to certain modifications of the original law. It was then accepted by the Filipinos, and finally, in March, 1935, a constitution was adopted for the Philippine Commonwealth. The United States had agreed to withdraw entirely in ten years with the only important stipulation, aside from the economic and political restrictions during the transitional period, the possible retention of a naval base.

Since 1900 our policy in the Far East had been characterized by successive changes of front. Again and again we had taken a strong stand only to back down when it became evident that our professed objectives could be achieved only by the application of forcible measures which the American people were not ready to support. But the retreat at this time carried us farther than on any previous occasion since the occupation of the Philippines.

The most valid explanation for this attitude was the growing popular realization that the importance of our national interests in the Orient had been greatly exaggerated. They might be worth protection by diplomacy; they were assuredly not worth protection by force. And since diplomacy had admittedly failed, the American people were no longer willing to run the risks which even threatened intervention entailed.

Both American trade and American investments in China had greatly increased since the declaration of the Open Door policy in 1900. The former had expanded by 1930 from some $32,000,000 to $226,000,000, marking a gain from 9.5 per cent to 16.5 per cent of China's total foreign trade. Investments, exclusive of mission property, had risen from $19,700,000 to $196,-800,000, an increase from 2.5 per cent to 6.1 per cent of all foreign investments in China. We were exporting large quantities of raw cotton, kerosene, and tobacco in return for various imports of which raw silk and tung oil were the most important commodities. Nevertheless, this trade was still less than 3 per cent of our total foreign commerce, and was exceeded in value by trade with at least six European and four Latin American countries, while the value of our investments in China was only about 1.3 per cent of our total foreign investments.

Furthermore our trade with China was considerably less than our trade with Japan. The latter had been valued somewhat higher even in 1900, but it was now twice as high. With exports aggregating $164,570,000, Japan had become our fourth best foreign market in 1930, while imports valued at $279,040,000 made her second only to Canada as a source of supplies.

In succeeding years the importance of the Japanese

market increased still further while that of China declined. In 1935 our exports to the former country totaled $203,260,000, and to the latter only $38,156,000. On this basis, Japan was buying more than five times as much in this country as China; indeed, her purchases were exceeded only by those of Great Britain and Canada. It would have been difficult, moreover, to discover any foreign trade on a generally less competitive basis. It consisted largely of an exchange of raw cotton for raw silk. The United States and Japan, Foreign Minister Hirota stated in the Diet on January 22, 1935, are bound "by a vital economic relationship of mutual interdependence unparalleled elsewhere."

Nevertheless, developments in this period might have followed a different course had the commercial and financial interests in this country been able to exert the pressure which they had exercised at other times in behalf of our economic stake in the Orient. But in the midst of a world-wide depression, with industry and finance on the defensive, there could be no effective revival of the economic imperialism of President McKinley, the dollar diplomacy of President Taft, or the forthright support for foreign trade of the Harding era. There was no strong force to battle in behalf of further protection of Chinese markets against Japanese encroachments.

It is impossible to say just how much these considerations actually influenced the Roosevelt Administration in adopting its general hands-off attitude toward Japanese imperialism. The economic motivation of foreign policy is easier to assume than prove. More important than trade was the sober realization, on political grounds, that there was no peaceful way whereby we could restrain Japan. Under the circumstances the "good neighbor" policy was not only the best policy but the only policy we could safely follow.

Every effort was made to emphasize our new cordiality. In an exchange of notes between the American Secretary of State and the Japanese Foreign Minister in February and March, 1934, Mr. Hull strongly emphasized the pacific relations between the two countries. "I believe that there are in fact no questions between our two countries," he said, "which, if they be viewed in proper perspective in both countries, can with any warrant be regarded as not readily susceptible to adjustment by pacific processes."

Upon declaration of Japan's ambitious Asiatic Monroe Doctrine just a month later, there was a great outcry in the American press. It was interpreted as transforming China into a vassal state, in flat repudiation of the Open Door. It clearly showed, the New York *Herald Tribune* said, that "no existing or contemplated treaty governing international relations in the Pacific, to which Japan is a signatory, is of the slightest value to any other signatory if there is any chance that it will prove an obstacle to a Japanese ambition." Nevertheless, nothing could have been more innocuous than the mild rejoinder emanating from Washington.

Forced to take some cognizance of the Japanese statement, the State Department merely reiterated that it was the opinion of the American people and the American Government that "no nation can, without the assent of the other nations concerned, rightfully endeavor to make conclusive its will in situations where there are involved the rights, the obligations and the legitimate interests of other sovereign states."

If Secretary Stimson's policy was not wholly abandoned, it was significantly toned down. We still stood on the record, which every Secretary of State since John Hay had endeavored to keep clear. But Japan could easily read between the lines that our interest in assertive measures for safeguarding either China's markets or her territorial integrity was at a very low ebb.

CHAPTER XVI

THE NAVAL ISSUE

IF PRESIDENT ROOSEVELT HAD THUS ADOPTED A FRIENDLY policy toward Japan which involved a laissez-faire attitude in regard to her operations in North China, his Administration at the same time reverted to a far more decisive attitude on naval questions. It gave early evidence that it had no intention of carrying its conciliatory program to the point of allowing Japan to attain in the Pacific area as a whole the supremacy she was establishing in Eastern Asia. This was demonstrated in March, 1934, a year after Roosevelt came into office, by passage of a bill providing a marked increase in naval appropriations.

The United States had not maintained its navy up to the limits set by the Washington and London Treaties during the previous Administrations of Hoover and Coolidge. It had allowed Japan to attain a strength well above the accepted ratios. Through enactment of the Vinson Act, which provided for the construction of sufficient new vessels to bring our navy up to its full quota by 1942, it now sought to make up for this advantage which Japan had gained. It also in effect served notice upon Japan that our more acquiescent attitude toward her continental policy did not by any means imply full confidence in her protestations that peace in the Orient was the sole objective of her foreign program.

The comparative naval strength of the two nations could not fail to become a problem of real concern after the events of 1931-32. There was as yet no actual armaments race, as there had been in 1921, to increase whatever tension might be caused by political developments. The restrictions of the naval limitation treaties were still in effect. But Japan was showing a restiveness under the enforced inequality of the provisions of those treaties which was expressed in a growing demand upon the part of the military and naval parties within the country for complete naval equality. While it was Secretary Stimson who had hinted that with violation of the political accords reached at Washington the basis for the naval treaties had been undermined, Japan was the nation prepared to question their continued validity on quite different grounds.

Her interpretation of the new situation which presented itself in 1934 was a simple one. With enlarged responsibilities for the maintenance of peace in the Orient, entirely regardless of any question as to whether these were not self-assumed responsibilities occasioned by her own repudiation of the principle of collective security, Japan felt herself more than ever entitled to a navy equal to that of any other Power. Furthermore, the technical development of naval science and the progress of aviation no longer afforded Japan, it was claimed, even the security which the 5-5-3 ratio had represented in 1921.

The principle of international equality, considered by itself, was also advanced as a compelling reason for granting Japan the right to have as large a navy as either America or Great Britain. The Japanese had greatly resented the refusal of the Western World to admit racial equality at the Versailles Conference; they had resented even more deeply the discriminatory provisions of our immigration law. There was the same feeling of popular dissatisfaction toward a lower naval ratio, and the Japanese navalists zealously played upon it to enforce their demand for equality.

"In the ratio system," Ambassador Saito declared in an address in November, 1934, "is involved the question of national dignity and prestige. No one has ever thought that, by granting Japan equality in naval strength, either the United States or the British Empire will begin to feel anxiety about their own national security. That is not the point. The fear appears to be that in that case there will be no knowing what actions Japan may take toward China and other parts of the Far East. . . . It is something which the Japanese susceptibility cannot tolerate; it is something to which no man with a sense of honor will remain reconciled."

Writing somewhat later in *Foreign Affairs*, Admiral Nomura also stated that the Japanese people had been dissatisfied with the ratio system from its inception. They had come to look upon it, he said, "as a stigma of inferiority which hardly tends to sustain Japan's position in the Far East."

If equality were granted, Japan then favored as great a reduction in naval strength as the other Powers would accept. She developed a strong case in favor of navies strictly limited to defensive purposes, with abolition of capital ships and aircraft carriers. She was able to assert upon the basis of such a program a measure of support for disarmament which went further than that of any other country. Ready to reduce her navy by half, Ambassador Saito said in the address already quoted, "Japan's foremost purpose is to provide for the security of all concerned, to reduce the financial burden of peoples, and to contribute to the establishment of peace which is the supreme need of this time."

The American position in opposition to that of Japan was that the naval ratios already agreed upon constituted the only practical method for naval limitation. Further reductions were impossible on any other basis. As opposed to the equality of armaments proposed by Japan, the new conception of equality of security was set forth. America was entitled to a larger navy than Japan because of geographical considerations which demanded the means to defend two coastlines and protect the Panama Canal.

Equality of armaments and equality of security were not only two different principles, according to this thesis; they were incompatible and contradictory. Other factors were held to be of equal if not greater importance than armaments in determining a nation's capacity for defense, and they necessarily dictated unequal navies if equality of security was to be assured. Granted our principle, we too were willing to support further reductions in existing strength. No less than Japan, we were dedicated to the cause of disarmament and the maintenance of world peace—on our own terms.

The underlying reasons for this conflicting stand on equality of armaments and equality of security were not brought out in the official statements made by American and Japanese spokesmen during 1934. They were playing to the gallery of world opinion. For neither nation primarily sought disarmament. Each was actually attempting to safeguard its own political interests. Japan sought the means to be able to defend not only her own shores but all of Asia against any possible interference; the United States sought at least the reserve power which would not leave her entirely without influence in the Orient.

On any other basis the respective positions of the two nations had no real validity. In view of the distance from its base at which an American fleet would have to operate, and the possible need to keep at least a part of our forces in the Atlantic, Japan could not reasonably claim that her national security was menaced by the superiority accorded this country through the Washington and London Treaties. Unless her ambition involved complete domination of the Western Pacific, she had nothing to fear. But by the same token, if her fleet were equal to that of the United States, she could effectively prevent any possible interference with her policy on the Asiatic mainland. The greater the reduction within a common upper limit, moreover, the more security Japan would have. Able to concentrate all her forces off the Asiatic Coast, she would have a superiority which no other Power could challenge.

On the other hand, even a fleet equal to the American fleet could not safely be dispatched to American waters. The defensive force to which Japan was willing to restrict her navy if a common upper limit was agreed upon, could never become a menace to continental United States. Our position thus implied the right to a navy stronger than was necessary simply to safeguard national security. It was to be at least a potential threat to Japan in the Western Pacific, should public opinion ever countenance possible support of the Open Door policy.

This was implied in many responsible statements. It was the definite assumption of naval authorities. In the annual report of the Secretary of Navy in 1933, our policy was expounded by the General Naval Board as maintenance of a navy "in sufficient strength to support the national policies and commerce" of the United States.

These were the vital factors in the controversy over naval power in the Pacific, however much they were beclouded by official argument. The attempt to resolve the controversy in the conversations held in London in the summer and autumn of 1934, never had any real chance of success. Even before they commenced, Japan let it be known that she was now so utterly opposed to the ratio system that she could never agree to it.

British efforts to discover a compromise between the American and Japanese points of view completely failed. Japan insisted upon her right to full equality through the establishment of a common upper limit for the American, British, and Japanese navies; America insisted upon retention of the ratios established at the Washington Conference. The deadlock was complete. When Great Britain swung toward support of the American principle—"In view of our greater range of responsibilities . . . ," said Sir John Simon, "a British navy that is comparatively larger is necessary in order to preserve in practice equality of security"—Japan finally prepared to terminate the Washington Treaty. The London conversations were thereupon adjourned, and on December 29, 1934, Tokyo formally notified the State Department of its decision.

This clearly enough presaged the complete collapse of the disarmament movement so hopefully initiated some thirteen years earlier, but termination of the treaty did not of itself preclude negotiation of some substitute. Japan carefully undertook to make this clear.

"The present step taken by the Japanese Government," the Foreign Office declared, "is only a logical outcome of our fundamental policy which aims at the conclusion of another pact to supersede the Washington Treaty. Our Government desire fervently to arrive at an agreement which is just and fair for all the parties concerned and entirely in accord with the spirit of disarmament. They are prepared, despite the termination of the Washington Treaty, to pursue with undiminished zeal friendly negotiations with the other powers."

Until the close of the ensuing year—1935—the naval issue remained somewhat in the background while both the American and Japanese Governments made consistent efforts to render international relations as smooth as possible. Statesmen on either side of the Pacific made repeated protestations of friendship and declared that war was unimaginable. There were frequent gestures of good-will.

Mrs. Roosevelt and Ambassador Saito happily characterized the cherry blossom as a symbol of friendship in April; Mayor LaGuardia of New York dispatched some life-size dolls on a good-will tour of Japan in June; and after some discussion as to whether he should take off his shoes in the presence of the Emperor, Vice-President Garner visited Tokyo in October to reaffirm the Administration's "good neighbor" policy. Possibly these manifestations of friendship served to assuage Japan's wounded feelings when the magazine *Vanity Fair* published a cartoon of the Japanese Emperor pulling a rickshaw, but they hardly constituted an effective contribution to any permanent solution of American-Japanese problems.

For despite cherry blossoms and life-size dolls, the persistent campaign of Japan to bring additional Chinese territory under her influence, and the activities of the military in North China, could not fail to arouse renewed concern both in Washington and among the American public as to how far Japan was going. Proponents of the Open Door considered American interests to be seriously endangered by this accumulating evidence that Manchukuo did not represent the full goal of Japanese ambitions. When in December the movement for autonomy in North China appeared to foreshadow the creation of a new state comparable to Manchukuo, if not the union of Manchukuo and the northern Chinese provinces into a great Japanese-dominated empire, the State Department felt compelled to make some statement.

It was not even as strong as the mild remonstrance made some twenty months earlier. There was no direct protest to Japan and no warning of any possible action on our part. Secretary Hull merely pointed out that the unusual developments taking place in North China were of concern to all the treaty Powers, and that in view of our interests in the area under reference, the American Government was "closely observing what is happening there." He strongly reiterated our faith in the sanctity of international agreements. "This government," he stated, "adheres to the provisions of the treaties to which it is a party and continues to bespeak respect by all nations for the provisions of the treaties solemnly entered into for the purpose of facilitating and regulating, to reciprocal and common advantage, the contacts between and among the countries signatory."

Japan's attitude was naturally not conducive to any change of heart in America in regard to naval policy. The Administration was stiffened in its resolve to maintain at all costs our right to naval superiority. If Japan refused to accept the ratio principle, it was considered wiser policy to allow her the freedom of action which would result from failure to conclude a new treaty. For in that event the United States too would retain freedom of action, and our greater resources would enable us to outbuild Japan in any prospective naval race. And however apathetic popular opinion had become in regard to maintenance of our political influence in the Far East, it gave the Administration full support in its refusal to weaken our relative naval power in the Pacific.

If there was some illogicality in pursuing a political policy which was marked by virtual abandonment of any pretense of upholding the Open Door, and a naval policy which insisted upon a fleet superiority which

could only be justified as necessary for possible intervention in Eastern Asia, the public easily ignored it.

We were preserving our rights against future eventualities. Whatever might be said of the impossibility of
Japan attacking the United States, the American people
could not accept the idea that she should, even in principle, be allowed a navy equal to our own. Since we
had the potential resources to outbuild Japan in any
prospective naval race, we intended to maintain the
right to do so.

Nor did anything which happened in 1935 in any
way serve to modify Japan's position. Admittedly failure
to persuade America to accept naval equality meant
defeat for her hopes of winning complete security for
the advancement of her continental policy. But the collapse of the disarmament negotiations would leave her
no worse off than she was under the treaty unless America took the initiative in starting a naval race. In any
event, the issue had been stressed too strongly for the
Japanese Government to be able to back down. National
pride was more directly involved than ever before.
Japanese public opinion insisted upon maintenance of
the right to equality whatever the possible consequences.

A comparison of the relative strength of the two
fleets in the summer of 1935 showed that of Japan to
be well above 70 per cent that of the United States.
While this country had 283,150 tons either under construction or appropriated for in contrast with 117,707
tons for Japan, this merely indicated that the latter
country had maintained its fleet up to treaty limits and
America had not. On the basis of total ships built, the
American navy was 1,084,910 tons and the Japanese

navy 748,997 tons; in respect to ships under age, these comparative figures were 731,510 tons and 648,415 tons.

Further indicative of the naval rivalry which even under treaty restrictions was beginning to replace the coöperative approach to limitation were the rising naval appropriations of the two nations. Those of the United States for the fiscal year 1936 had attained a new peacetime record of $460,000,000, and while Japan's were very much lower, due both to a smaller number of ships building and to lower maintenance costs, the comparable figure of $159,000,000 also represented a new high figure. Both Powers had adopted programs of marked expansion, and were also developing to an even greater extent their naval air forces.

It was under these conditions, Japan aggressively pursuing her imperialistic policy in the Far East, and both Japan and America enlarging their naval forces to the maximum and spending vast sums on their increased efficiency, that 1935 drew to a close. The situation in many respects paralleled that which had prevailed in 1921. Again a naval conference was summoned, but this time in a far different spirit. In the earlier year it had been called with a firm resolve upon the part of the participating nations, although Japan came somewhat reluctantly, to work out both the political and naval problems of the Pacific. In 1935 it was held almost perfunctorily, and probably would not have been held at all, had not the expiring Washington Treaty stipulated that such negotiations should take place.

In the intervening years the entire world, not only Japan, had completely retraced the steps which had been taken along the road to collective security and general disarmament. As the conference prepared to meet, the press was reporting on Germany's rearmament in violation of the Versailles Treaty, and Italy's attack upon Abyssinia in violation of the Kellogg Pact, as well as upon Japan's continued disregard of her obligations under the Nine Power Treaty.

The basic difference in regard to the situation in the Pacific, however, was that America could not hope to exercise the pressure upon Japan which she had been able to exert in 1921. At the Washington Conference, this country compelled Japan to surrender the gains she had made on the Asiatic mainland during the World War and forced her to accept an inferior navy. The national temper, our naval strength, and the support of the other Powers enabled us to threaten Japan with a diplomatic isolation which she did not dare risk. Fourteen years later a Japan which had taken advantage of world absorption in other problems to renew the march of imperialism could defy America to call her to account. We were no longer prepared to take an aggressive stand in favor of the Open Door; we had failed to maintain our naval strength; and there was no support from the other Powers for any effective program to restrain Japan.

In 1935 we were reaping the rewards of forcing upon Japan a settlement of Pacific problems which afforded no adequate recognition of what she considered her legitimate rights, and at the same time failing to provide any means to enforce compliance with that settlement.

We had relied upon voluntary collective action for maintaining the peace of the Pacific without assuring ourselves that it was to the general interest of Japan to uphold such peace. It was too late for the concessions which once might have established real stability in the Orient. There was no denying the tragic reversion to the politics of power for which, it had been so hopefully believed, the Washington Conference had substituted a new order of international good-will.

Under the circumstances a wholly defeatist attitude prevailed in London. As in the preliminary conversations a year earlier, efforts were made to reconcile the conflicting views of the United States and Japan, but at no time was there any general belief that they could possibly succeed. Japan presented her case for what was termed "a state of non-menace and non-aggression," to be secured by agreement upon a common upper limit for naval construction with either total abolition or drastic reduction of all offensive types of vessels. America and Great Britain stood out firmly against any modification of the existing ratios. They provided as nearly as was humanly possible, Norman Davis stated, an equilibrium of defense and an equality of security which the United States could not give up under any circumstances.

It became merely a question of when the point would be reached when Japan would withdraw from the conference. The world paid little attention to the largely academic discussions in which the delegates debated equality of security and equality of armaments. It was generally accepted that the Japanese demands logically followed the assertion of Japanese political supremacy in the Far East and that effective naval limitation was doomed.

Formal notice of withdrawal from the conference was

given on January 15, 1936. "As it has become sufficiently clear at today's session of the First Committee
that the basic principles embodied in our proposals for
comprehensive limitation and reduction of naval armaments cannot secure general support," the Japanese
stated, "our delegation has now come to the conclusion
we can no longer usefully continue our participation in
deliberations of the present conference."

For so long had this action been foreseen, and so
reconciled had public opinion come to the breakdown
of naval disarmament, that Japan's move caused little
stir. The political complications of Europe had led the
world almost to the brink of war, and this new demonstration of the instability of international affairs appeared only a minor incident in world-wide unrest.

The conference continued in session after Japan's
withdrawal. Despite a series of further crises in European politics, the delegations of the United States, Great
Britain, France, and Italy patiently tried to discover
a formula to save something from the wreck of past
hopes. In the end Italy too dropped out, but late in
March a treaty was finally signed by the three other
Powers wherein they accepted limitations upon certain
types of naval vessels and undertook to exchange advance information as to their building programs.

Without any agreement whatsoever for quantitative
limitation or reduction of their navies, and without the
participation of Japan, this treaty remained a pale
shadow of the one it replaced. Possibly more important
than any of its carefully reserved provisions was the
exchange of letters, coincident with signature of the
treaty, between the British Foreign Secretary, Anthony

Eden, and our principal delegate, Norman Davis, which served to reaffirm the solidarity of British and American naval policy in the Pacific. The two statesmen agreed in behalf of their governments that there would be "no competitive building as between ourselves and that the principle of parity as between the fleets of the members of the British Commonwealth and the United States shall continue unchanged."

There was no reference to Japan in this exchange of letters. But it could be clearly understood that in the event she began to increase her navy beyond the old ratio, both England and America were prepared to maintain their superiority by concerted action.

The prospects of a naval race developing as a result of the collapse of the ratio system were minimized on all sides. In both the United States and Japan, any idea of competitive building was formally denied. Yet at the same time, both nations immediately sought still higher naval appropriations. The big navy advocates of either country were soon pointing to the activities of the other Power as sufficient cause for demanding still more extensive building programs.

In Tokyo, the Minister of the Navy stated that the American program and its potential threat to Japanese policy in Asia proved the need for additional appropriations for national defense. In Washington, the chairman of the Senate Foreign Relations Committee vehemently attacked Japanese policy as prejudicial to our interests. "Congress will not be bulldozed," he said, "into the abandonment of our national defense, the protection of our legitimate foreign trade, or our commerce with China."

With the expiration of the naval treaties on December 31, 1936, an epoch in the relations between America and Japan came to an end. Conditions in the Pacific and the Far East could hardly have presented, on this important date, a more striking contrast to those prevailing at the opening of the century.

In 1900 America was in the heyday of imperialistic fervor. We had occupied the Philippines to ensure our political supremacy in the Pacific and sponsored the Open Door policy to safeguard our rights in what was believed to be the all-important commerce of China. We had made ourselves the self-appointed champion of Chinese political and territorial integrity. And in that year Japan still remained in the international background, an innocent onlooker of foreign affairs, whose latent ambitions were carefully disguised. She was far too weak to exercise any decisive influence on the course of events in the Orient, and so far from challenging American naval power in the Pacific that even the possibility of such a contingency was not foreseen. The traditional friendship between the two Powers on either side of the Pacific was still untroubled by any idea of potential conflict.

Thirty-six years later, America had apparently said farewell to imperialism. We had agreed to surrender our sovereignty over the Philippines and tacitly admitted the practical failure of our policy to maintain the Open Door and preserve China's territorial integrity. While we still insisted upon the right to a navy superior to that of Japan, the goal of acknowledged supremacy over the Pacific had long since been given up. In this same period Japan had extended her Empire to the Asiatic mainland, successfully challenged the basic conception of the Open Door, and vigorously asserted in principle her right to full naval equality with America.

This decline in the influence of America and rise in the power of Japan represented what it is now easy to recognize as the almost inevitable consequence of a conflict of policies in which the interests of the one nation were so much more vitally involved than those of the other. The situation in 1936 reflected the triumph of Japan's aggressive program for Asiatic expansion over our vacillating stand in behalf of the Open Door.

It was, indeed, far easier to understand why America had found herself increasingly unwilling to carry her opposition to Japanese policies to the point where it could be truly effective, than to justify the negatively obstructive attitude we had for so long maintained. For the extent of our trade and investments in China does not afford any valid reason, touching upon national interest, for active intervention in their support, and a largely sentimental enthusiasm for China's independence, even though it had led us in the past to promise more than we were prepared to deliver, can hardly be held sufficent warrant for incurring the risks of war in its defense.

It is sometimes maintained that a stronger impulse behind our historic policy in the Far East has been the belief that an independent China is our best protection against a too powerful Japan. The vague fear that some day Japan may actually threaten our national security runs persistently throughout the history of our relations with her in the past thirty years. Alarmists are continually predicting that through control not only of North China but of all Eastern Asia, Japan will eventually dominate the entire Pacific area and hold America almost at her mercy.

This vague fear bears little relation to the realities of Far Eastern politics. Whatever Japan's ambitions for expansion in Asia, there are no rational grounds to believe that she would ever look farther afield. Japanese militarists have always proved practical-minded. Before the Diet, on January 21, 1936, Foreign Minister Hirota stated the theory which his country has always hoped America would eventually accept as the final determinant in reconciling the American-Japanese conflict. "Since Japan and America are geographically so situated that they possess each a special sphere of activity of their own," he said, "it is impossible that the two nations should ever come to a collision."

No foreign policy, in any event, could appear more futile for the United States than one which might invite war in the Orient today in order to guard against these chimerical fears of a distant tomorrow. Our defense against an imperialistic Japan looking for new fields to conquer is the immense barrier of the Pacific Ocean.

In its possible bearing upon the Far East, the Permanent Neutrality Bill signed by President Roosevelt on May 1, 1937, would appear to go far toward accepting the Japanese thesis of exclusive spheres of interest. Despite such obligations as we have assumed in the past for supporting Chinese sovereignty, there is no exception in its provisions, as in the case of the Latin American Republics, to maintenance of a strict aloofness in the case of any attack upon China. The Act prohibits the export of arms, ammunition, and implements of war to any belligerent, and at the President's discretion provides for the extension of such an embargo to additional articles or materials unless they are transported in other than American vessels and unless all right, title, and interest in them has previously passed to some foreign government or agency. In their practical application it is patent that these provisions might materially aid Japan in warfare against China because of a command of war materials and facilities for trade which China completely lacks.

Nevertheless, it cannot be categorically stated that our policy in the Far East has become one of complete withdrawal. The doctrine promulgated by Secretary Hay at the opening of the century has signally failed, but it does not necessarily follow that such failure is fully accepted by either the American Government or the American people. Our anti-war program was not adopted with the Far East in mind, and the force of tradition is strong. Against the evidence afforded by the neutrality law and our passive attitude toward current Japanese operations in North China, must be set certain other factors. Our continued refusal to recognize Manchukuo, the development of strategically important aerial routes across the Pacific, and insistence upon a naval superiority over Japan which can be justified only by the possible need to protect our interests in the Western Pacific rather than by the demands of self-defense, serve in part to nullify the implications of our present laissez-faire attitude. Although nothing in the field of foreign affairs would appear more important than the definite determination of just where we stand, the bases of our policy in regard to future developments in the Orient remain obscure.

BIBLIOGRAPHICAL NOTES

WHILE THE APPENDED LIST OF SOURCES—REPRESENTING only a limited selection of the books dealing with American-Japanese relations in the twentieth century— comprises the basic material upon which the author has relied for this historical study, perhaps some further account might be given of how these sources have been used.

Primary reliance has been placed upon such official documents as are available, letters and memoirs of the principal actors upon the international stage, and contemporary comment culled from newspapers and magazines. The period under review is too recent for fully adequate material in the first two categories: the diplomatic correspondence has not all been published, and comparatively few volumes of letters and memoirs have appeared. The annual volumes of *Papers Relating to the Foreign Relations of the United States,* however, carry the story through 1921; *Senate Document 126* (67th Congress, 2d Session) is the official account of the Conference on the Limitation of Armament; *Senate Document 55* (72nd Congress, 1st Session), entitled "Conditions in Manchuria," contains official correspondence between the United States and Japan, together with other documents, for the period from September, 1931, through January, 1932, and valuable material is contained in the *Report of the Commission of Enquiry Appointed by the League of Nations* (Lytton Report) issued in 1932.

Treaties and other documents may also be found in J. V. A. MacMurray's *Treaties and Agreements With and Concerning China;* W. W. Willoughby's *Foreign Rights and Interests in China;* and various year books. A convenient source for the correspondence and minutes of the League of Nations is W. W. Willoughby's *The Sino-Japanese Controversy and the League of Nations.* Official correspondence not appearing in any of these publications has been largely taken from releases of the Department of State or the New York *Times.*

Letters and memoirs of direct importance include those of John Hay, Theodore Roosevelt, Woodrow Wilson, Colonel E. M. House, Robert Lansing, and Henry L. Stimson among the Americans; those of Count Hayashi and Viscount Ishii among the Japanese.

Newspaper comment has been almost entirely taken from the *Literary Digest,* except for the most recent years, and other evidences of contemporary opinion from periodicals and current books. The number of such articles and books is legion, especially in periods of tension between the United States and Japan. While they do not always present reliable historical material, they are important as reflecting a contemporary point of view. Special note should be made, however, of authoritative articles in the 1930 edition of *American Foreign Relations,* issued by the Council on Foreign Relations, and other publications of this organization, notably the magazine *Foreign Affairs;* various studies of the Institute of Pacific Relations and its biannual volume on *Problems of the Pacific;* the July, 1933, issue of the *Annals of the American Academy of Political and Social Science;* the reports on the Far East of the Foreign Policy Association, and certain special articles in *Contemporary Japan, Asia, Pacific Affairs,* and the *Far Eastern Review.* No attempt has been made to list these special studies and magazine articles in the bibliography.

The author is also greatly indebted to a number of general histories of the Far East and to many special studies on specific phases of American-Japanese relations to which subsequent reference will be made. He would particularly single out, however, three books by Tyler Dennett: *Americans in Eastern Asia, Roosevelt and the Russo-Japanese War,* and *John Hay;* the volume on *Far Eastern International Relations* by Hosea Ballou Morse and Harley

Farnsworth MacNair; Thomas A. Bailey's *Theodore Roosevelt and the Japanese-American Crisis;* Payson J. Treat's *Japan and the United States;* and *War and Diplomacy in the Japanese Empire* by Tatsuji Takeuchi.

For the chapter on imperialism, the author has relied upon a work of his own in this field, *America in the Pacific,* from which the quotations on the popular reaction to our expansionist activities are largely taken, and various general histories of Japan, notably that of William Montgomery McGovern. *Beveridge and the Progressive Era* by Claude G. Bowers and *Our Times: the Turn of the Century* by Mark Sullivan further indicate the hold of imperialism on public opinion during this period, while E. P. Dean's article on "The Expansion of Japanese Rule," in the April, 1935, issue of *Foreign Affairs,* is a brief but useful study of this topic. The Japanese statements on national expansion are quoted from *Far Eastern International Relations;* Senator Beveridge's interview with Prince Ito from *Beveridge and the Progressive Era.*

The account of the formulation of the Open Door Doctrine and of American policy during the Boxer Rebellion is derived primarily from the appropriate volumes of *Foreign Relations,* to which more exact reference does not appear necessary. Every writer dealing with this question, however, is greatly indebted to Tyler Dennett's careful research, as brought out in his life of John Hay, and to that of A. L. P. Dennis in *Adventures in American Diplomacy 1896-1906.* The record of early American commerce in the Far East is taken from the author's *The Old China Trade.* An interesting contemporary survey of conditions in the Far East is found in *The Problem of Asia,* by Captain Alfred Thayer Mahan, while note should also be made of *The Open Door Doctrine* by M. J. Bau and *The Boxer Rebellion* by Paul H. Clements. Newspaper comment is quoted from the *Literary Digest.*

The chapter dealing with the Russo-Japanese War is based upon Dennett's *Roosevelt and the Russo-Japanese War* and Dennis's *Adventures in American Diplomacy.*

The life of Roosevelt by Joseph Bucklin Bishop was also helpful and provided the quotations from Roosevelt's letters. On the origins of the Anglo-Japanese Alliance, see Dennis's *The Anglo-Japanese Alliance*.

For the aftermath of the Russo-Japanese War and change in American public opinion toward Japan, contemporary newspaper comment, as reported in the *Literary Digest*, and magazine articles provided the principal sources of material. The Roosevelt biographies were again useful for their evidence of the President's attitude, while a comprehensive survey of the events recorded in this chapter is found in *Theodore Roosevelt and the Japanese-American Crisis* by Thomas A. Bailey.

The period of dollar diplomacy is most graphically recorded in Herbert Croly's life of Willard Straight, but the volumes of *Foreign Relations* for the period 1909-13 contain a wealth of basic material. A great deal of this is more conveniently available in Willoughby's *Foreign Rights and Interests in China*, while a valuable study of the period is G. A. Finch's article on "American Diplomacy and the Financing of China" in the *American Journal of International Law*, 1916. The rôle of E. H. Harriman is recorded in *E. H. Harriman's Far Eastern Policy* by George Kennan. See also *The Idea of National Interest* by Charles A. Beard.

Developments in the Far East during the World War have been based on a wide variety of sources. The authority for the discussion of Japan's decision to occupy Tsingtao is *War and Diplomacy in the Japanese Empire* by Tatsuji Takeuchi; the reaction in China is taken from *An American Diplomat in China* by Paul S. Reinsch. American notes of the period are found in the appropriate volumes of *Foreign Relations*. While valuable material upon the popular attitude of this country is found in Sidney L. Gulick's *Anti-Japanese War Scare* and Jabez T. Sunderland's *Rising Japan*, the best sources are the contemporary newspaper and magazine articles which are far too numerous to list. The quotation on the cabinet discussion of the possibility of war is taken from Ray Stannard Baker's *Woodrow Wil-*

son: Life and Letters, and the material on the Twenty-One Demands from Willoughby's *Foreign Rights and Interests in China.* The speeches of Viscount Ishii on his visit to America may be found in *The Imperial Japanese Mission— 1917,* issued by the Carnegie Endowment for International Peace, but for the negotiations leading up to the Lansing-Ishii Agreement, the two indispensable sources are Lansing's *War Memoirs* and Viscount Ishii's *Diplomatic Commentaries.*

The material for the chapter on the Versailles Conference has been taken from Baker's *Woodrow Wilson and World Settlement,* Vol. 2, Lansing's *The Peace Negotiations,* Charles Seymour's edition of *The Intimate Papers of Colonel House,* and Takeuchi's *War and Diplomacy in the Japanese Empire.* Newspaper comment is again taken from the *Literary Digest;* the statement of Henry Cabot Lodge from the *Congressional Record* (66th Congress, 1st Session), Vol. 58, p. 6878.

A number of books deal with the strange episode of Allied intervention in Siberia, notably *America's Siberian Adventure* by General William S. Graves, the commander of the American forces, *Trailing the Bolsheviki* by Carl W. Ackerman, an American correspondent, *Siberia Today* by Frederick Moore, *The Far Eastern Republic* by Henry K. Norton, and *American Policy Toward Russia Since 1917* by Frederick Lewis Schuman. The account of President Wilson's decision is taken from *The Intimate Papers of Colonel House,* the official correspondence largely quoted from the Senate Document on the *Conference on Limitation of Armament,* and discussion of the attitude of Japan is primarily based upon *War and Diplomacy in the Japanese Empire.*

For the period between the Versailles Conference and the Washington Conference, contemporary newspaper and magazine articles, together with the *Congressional Record,* constitute a primary source for which there is no substitute, while the course of the conference negotiations in 1921-22 is officially reported in the previously noted *Senate*

Document. Three books on the Washington Conference might also be mentioned, each expressing a very definite viewpoint: Mark Sullivan's optimistic and picturesque account, *The Great Adventure at Washington,* the more realistic study of Raymond Leslie Buell, and Yamato Ichihashi's *The Washington Conference and After.* Newspapers afford the best evidence of public opinion.

A number of pertinent articles in *Foreign Affairs* afforded valuable material for the first section of the chapter on the Era of Good Feeling: "The Far Eastern Situation Since the Washington Conference," by Kenneth Scott Latourette (1922), "The Difficulties and Hopes of Japan," by Yusuke Tsurumi (1924), "The Situation in the Far East," anonymous (1929), and several articles by K. K. Kawakami, to whose presentation of the Japanese point of view throughout this entire period, in both books and magazine articles, previous reference might well have been made. For the immigration controversy, reference was had to the *Annals of the American Academy of Political and Social Science,* 1921; Raymond Leslie Buell's *Japanese Immigration,* a World Peace Foundation pamphlet; R. D. McKenzie's *Oriental Exclusion,* issued by the Institute of Pacific Relations; and Yamato Ichihashi's *Japanese in the United States.* For events in the Far East the author relied upon such general accounts as that of Morse and MacNair, *China's Foreign Relations* by Robert T. Pollard, and *The Chinese Revolution* by Arthur N. Holcombe. Japan's position at the London Naval Conference is most thoroughly discussed by Takeuchi.

While the background for events in Manchuria has been derived from a synthesis of various sources, the most important individual study of modern Japanese foreign policy is *The Basis of Japanese Foreign Policy* by Albert E. Hindmarsh. *Japan's Special Position in Manchuria* and *The International Relations of Manchuria,* both by Carl Walter Young, are outstanding studies of this topic; *Japan's Economic Position* by John E. Orchard and *Japan* by Harold G. Moulton are valuable discussions of

Japanese economics; *Japanese Government and Politics* by Harold Scott Quigley is important for its account of the subjects expressed in the title; and the population problem is most adequately reviewed in E. F. Penrose's *Population Theories and Their Application with Special Reference to Japan*. The Lytton Report, of course, contains valuable material on this general subject, while there are numerous books and magazine articles by Japanese apologists for their country's foreign policy. See for example, "America Teaches, Japan Learns," by K. K. Kawakami in the January, 1932, issue of the *Atlantic Monthly*.

For actual events in Manchuria in 1931 and the international negotiations which they occasioned, the Lytton Report, *Senate Document 55* on "Conditions in Manchuria," *The Sino-Japanese Controversy and the League of Nations, War and Diplomacy in the Japanese Empire, The Far Eastern Crisis* by Henry L. Stimson, and contemporary newspaper accounts have provided the essential material. Official statements are quoted from the government documents, newspaper comment from the *Literary Digest*. Ambassador Matsuoka's statement is taken from Willoughby.

In the two final chapters, those dealing with developments since 1931, authoritative sources are naturally inadequate, and reliance has necessarily been placed to a marked degree upon newspaper accounts and magazine articles. As indicative of popular interest in the question of American-Japanese relations, some 87 articles on this topic are listed in the *Reader's Guide to Periodical Literature* for the period between July, 1932, and June, 1935. As important reflections of the Japanese point of view, note should be taken of *Japan's Policies and Purposes*, a collection of the speeches of the Japanese ambassador to the United States, issued in 1935; "Permanent Bases of Japanese Foreign Policy," by Viscount Ishii, in *Foreign Affairs*, January, 1933; "The Aims of Japan," by Baron Wakatsuki, also in *Foreign Affairs*, July, 1935, and "Peace in the Pacific," by Iyesato Tokugawa, in *Contemporary Japan*, September, 1933. Comparable statements of American policy are contained in *The Far Eastern Crisis,* by Henry L. Stimson, and "American Foreign Policy," by Norman Davis, in *Foreign Affairs,* (supplement) January, 1934, while among other magazine articles are "American and Japanese Relations," by William R. Castle, Jr., in the *Far Eastern Review,* July, 1934; "America and Japanese Aims," by Tyler Dennett, in *Current History,* March, 1934; "Japan's Challenge to American Policy," by Nicholas Roosevelt, in *Asia,* February, 1935, and "The Realistic Foreign Policy of Japan," by A. E. Hindmarsh, in *Foreign Affairs,* January, 1935. See also the collection of articles in the July, 1933, *Annals of the American Academy of Political and Social Science.*

For the movement to grant the Philippine Islands their independence, the author has relied largely upon his own study, "The Philippines and the Hare-Hawes-Cutting Act," a report of the Foreign Policy Association, January 3, 1934, and Grayson L. Kirk's recent book, *Philippine Independence.* Statistics on American trade and investments in China are from Charles F. Remer's *Foreign Investments in China* and the *Statistical Abstract of the United States.*

The naval issue has been discussed on the basis of negotiations and public statements as reported in the press, quotations being taken from the New York *Times,* while the review of the comparative naval strength of America and Japan is based upon the July, 1935, statement of the Office of Naval Intelligence, as quoted in the *Foreign Policy Report* on "The End of Naval Disarmament" by David H. Popper, October 23, 1935. A provocative study of this question is *The Future of Naval Power in the Pacific,* by Walter Millis. Among important magazine articles setting forth the position of the two countries are "Disarmament Problems," by Norman Davis, *Foreign Affairs* (supplement), April, 1935; "Pending Naval Questions," by Admiral William V. Pratt, *Foreign Affairs,* April, 1935; "Japan's Case for Sea Power," by G. Sekine, *Current History,* November, 1934, and "Japan's Demand for Naval Equality," by Admiral Kichisaburo Nomura, *Foreign Affairs,* January, 1935.

Selected Sources

ABBOTT, JAMES FRANCIS—*Japanese Expansion and American Policies* (New York, 1916).

ACKERMAN, CARL W.—*Trailing the Bolsheviki* (New York, 1919).

American Foreign Relations, Survey of, Council on Foreign Relations (1928-31).

American Secretaries of State and Their Diplomacy, The, Vols. 9 and 10 (New York, 1929).

BAILEY, THOMAS A.—*Theodore Roosevelt and the Japanese-American Crisis* (Stanford, 1934).

BAKER, RAY STANNARD—*Woodrow Wilson: Life and Letters* (New York, 1931).

—— *Woodrow Wilson and World Settlement,* Vol. 2 (New York, 1922).

BALLARD, G. A.—*The Influence of the Sea on the Political History of Japan* (London, 1921).

BARNES, JOSEPH, Editor—*Empire in the East* (New York, 1934).

BAU, M. J.—*The Open Door Doctrine* (New York, 1923).

BEARD, CHARLES A.—*The Idea of National Interest* (New York, 1934).

BISHOP, JOSEPH BUCKLIN—*Theodore Roosevelt and His Times,* 2 vols. (New York, 1920).

BLAKESLEE, GEORGE H.—*Japan and Japanese-American Relations* (New York, 1912).

BOWERS, CLAUDE G.—*Beveridge and the Progressive Era* (Boston, 1932).

BUELL, RAYMOND LESLIE—*Japanese Immigration,* World Peace Foundation Pamphlets, Vol. 7 (Boston, 1932).

—— *The Washington Conference* (New York, 1922).

BYWATER, HECTOR C.—*Sea Power in the Pacific* (London, 1934).

CARNEGIE ENDOWMENT FOR INTERNATIONAL PEACE—*The Imperial Japanese Mission—1917* (Washington, 1918).

China Year Book (Shanghai, 1934).

CLARK, GROVER—*A Place in the Sun* (New York, 1936).

—— *Economic Rivalries in China* (New Haven, 1932).

—— *The Balance Sheet of Imperialism* (New York, 1936).

CLEMENTS, PAUL H.—*The Boxer Rebellion* (New York, 1915).

CLYDE, PAUL H.—*Japan's Pacific Mandate* (New York, 1935).

Conditions in Manchuria, Senate Document 55, 72nd Congress, 1st Session (Washington, 1932).

CONDLIFFE, J. B., Editor—*Problems of the Pacific, 1927, 1929* (Chicago).

CONFERENCE ON THE LIMITATION OF ARMAMENT, *Senate Document 126, 67th Congress, 2nd Session* (Washington, 1922).

CROLY, HERBERT—*Willard Straight* (New York, 1924).

DENNETT, TYLER—*Americans in Eastern Asia* (New York, 1922).
——— *John Hay* (New York, 1933).
——— *Roosevelt and the Russo-Japanese War* (New York, 1925).
DENNIS, ALFRED L. P.—*Adventures in American Diplomacy 1896-1906* (New York, 1928).
——— *The Anglo-Japanese Alliance,* University of California Publications, Vol. 1, No. 1 (Berkeley, 1923).
DULLES, FOSTER RHEA—*America in the Pacific* (Boston, 1932).
——— *The Old China Trade* (Boston, 1930).

FIELD, F. V.—*Economic Handbook of the Pacific Area* (New York, 1934).
Foreign Relations of the United States, Papers Relating to, 1899-1920 (Washington).

GRAVES, WILLIAM S.—*America's Siberian Adventure* (New York, 1931).
GULICK, SIDNEY L.—*Anti-Japanese War Scare Stories* (New York, 1917).
——— *Toward Understanding Japan* (New York, 1935).

HARRIMAN, E. H., *see* KENNAN, GEORGE.
HAY, JOHN, *see* DENNETT, TYLER and THAYER, WILLIAM ROSCOE.
HAYASHI, COUNT—*Secret Memoirs,* edited by A. M. POOLEY (New York, 1915).
HEARN, LAFCADIO—*Japan: An Interpretation* (New York, 1924).
HINDMARSH, ALBERT E.—*The Basis of Japanese Foreign Policy* (Cambridge, 1936).
HOLCOMBE, ARTHUR N.—*The Chinese Revolution* (Cambridge, 1930).
HORNBECK, STANLEY K.—*Contemporary Politics in the Far East* (New York, 1916).
House, Colonel, The Intimate Papers of, edited by CHARLES SEYMOUR, Vols. 3 and 4 (Boston, 1928).

ICHIHASHI, YAMATO—*Japanese in the United States* (Stanford, 1932).
——— *The Washington Conference and After* (Stanford, 1928.)
ISHII, VISCOUNT KIKUJIRO—*Diplomatic Commentaries* (Baltimore, 1935).

Japan-Manchoukuo Year Book (Tokyo, 1934-35).
Japan Year Book, Foreign Affairs Association of Japan (Tokyo, 1933-35).

KAWAKAMI, K. K.—*American-Japanese Relations* (New York, 1912).
——— *Japan in World Politics* (New York, 1917).
——— *Japan's Pacific Policy* (New York, 1922).
——— *Japan Speaks* (New York, 1932).
——— *Manchoukuo, Child of Conflict* (New York, 1933).
KENNAN, GEORGE—*E. H. Harriman, A Biography* (New York, 1922).

KENNAN, GEORGE—*E. H. Harriman's Far Eastern Policy* (New York, 1917).

KIRK, GRAYSON L.—*Philippine Independence* (New York, 1936).

LANGER, WILLIAM L.—*The Diplomacy of Imperialism, 1890-1902.* 2 Vols. (New York, 1935).

LANSING, ROBERT—*The Peace Negotiations* (Boston, 1921).

Lansing, Robert, War Memoirs of (New York, 1935).

LASKER, BRUNO, and HOLLAND, W. L., Editors—*Problems of the Pacific, 1931, 1933* (Chicago),

LATANE, J. H.—*A History of American Foreign Policy* (New York, 1934).

LATOURETTE, KENNETH SCOTT—*A History of Christian Missions in China* (New York, 1929).

LATTIMORE, OWEN—*Manchuria—Cradle of Conflict* (New York, 1932).

LIPPMANN, WALTER—*The United States in World Affairs, 1931-35* (New York).

Lytton Report—*Report of the Commission of Enquiry Appointed by the League of Nations,* Department of State (Washington, 1932).

MACMURRAY, J. V. A.—*Treaties and Agreements With and Concerning China,* 2 vols. (New York, 1921).

MAHAN, ALFRED THAYER—*The Problem of Asia* (Boston, 1900).

Manchuria Year Book (Tokyo, 1931).

MCGOVERN, WILLIAM MONTGOMERY—*Modern Japan* (London, 1920).

MCKENZIE, R. D.—*Oriental Exclusion,* Institute of Pacific Relations (New York, 1927).

MILLARD, THOMAS F.—*America and the Far Eastern Question* (New York, 1909).

—— *Our Eastern Question* (New York, 1917).

MILLIS, WALTER—*The Future of Sea Power in the Pacific* (New York, 1935).

MOORE, FREDERICK—*Siberia Today* (New York, 1919).

MORSE, HOSEA BALLOU, and MACNAIR, HARLEY FARNSWORTH—*Far Eastern International Relations* (Boston, 1931).

MOULTON, HAROLD G.—*Japan* (Washington, 1931).

NITOBE, INAZO—*Japan* (London, 1931).

NORTON, HENRY K.—*The Far Eastern Republic of Siberia* (London, 1923).

ORCHARD, JOHN E.—*Japan's Economic Position* (New York, 1930).

PEFFER, NATHANIEL—*Must We Fight in Asia?* (New York, 1935).

PENROSE, E. F.—*Food Supply and Raw Materials in Japan* (Chicago, 1930).

PENROSE, E. F.—*Population Theories and Their Application with Special Reference to Japan* (Stanford, 1934).

POLLARD, ROBERT T.—*China's Foreign Relations* (New York, 1933).

POOLEY, A. M.—*Japan's Foreign Policies* (London, 1920).

PRINGLE, HENRY F.—*Theodore Roosevelt* (New York, 1931).

QUIGLEY, HAROLD SCOTT—*Japanese Government and Politics* (New York, 1932).

REINSCH, PAUL S.—*An American Diplomat in China* (New York, 1922).

REMER, CHARLES FREDERICK—*Foreign Investments in China* (New York, 1933).

ROOSEVELT, THEODORE, *see* BISHOP, JOSEPH BUCKLIN, *and* PRINGLE, HENRY F.

Royal Institute of International Affairs, *Survey*, 1924-36 (London).

SAITO, HIROSI—*Japan's Policies and Purposes* (Boston, 1935).

SCHUMAN, FREDERICK LEWIS—*American Policy Toward Russia Since 1917* (New York, 1928).

SEARS, LOUIS MARTIN—*A History of American Foreign Relations* (New York, 1935).

Statistical Abstract of the United States, Department of Commerce (Washington, 1935).

STIMSON, HENRY L.—*The Far Eastern Crisis* (New York, 1936).

STRAIGHT, WILLARD, *see* CROLY, HERBERT

SULLIVAN, MARK—*Our Times: the Turn of the Century* (New York, 1926).

—— *The Great Adventure at Washington* (New York, 1922).

SUNDERLAND, JABEZ T.—*Rising Japan* (New York, 1918).

TAFT, HENRY W.—*Japan and America* (New York, 1932).

TAKEUCHI, TATSUJI—*War and Diplomacy in the Japanese Empire* (New York, 1935).

THAYER, WILLIAM ROSCOE—*The Life and Letters of John Hay*, 2 vols. (Boston, 1915).

TOKUTOMI, IICHIRO—*Japanese-American Relations* (New York, 1922).

TREAT, PAYSON J.—*Diplomatic Relations between the United States and Japan, 1853-95* (Stanford, 1932).

—— *Japan and the United States* (Stanford, 1928).

—— *The Far East* (New York, 1928).

VAN DORN, HAROLD ARCHER—*Twenty Years of the Chinese Republic* (New York, 1932).

WASHINGTON CONFERENCE, *see* CONFERENCE ON THE LIMITATION OF ARMAMENT.

WILDES, H. E.—*Japan in Crisis* (New York, 1934).

WILLOUGHBY, W. W.—*Foreign Rights and Interests in China*, 2 vols. (Baltimore, 1927).

—— *The Sino-Japanese Controversy and the League of Nations* (Baltimore, 1935).

WILSON, WOODROW, *see* BAKER, RAY STANNARD.

YAKHONTOFF, VICTOR A.—*Russia and the Soviet Union in the Far East* (New York, 1931).

YOUNG, CARL WALTER—*The International Relations of Manchuria* (Chicago, 1929).

—— *Japan's Special Position in Manchuria* (Baltimore, 1931).

INDEX